The True Story of a
Not So Crazy Cat Lady

Catherine Walker

First Edition 2014

ISBN-13: 978-1502819659

ISBN-10: 1502819651

For my family,
          those with four legs as well as two.

ONE

They came into my life, quite by chance, the same week as my husband walked out of it. I'd dragged myself out of the house to stock up on ice cream, chocolate and DVD rentals and although it was May, the sun seemed about as enthusiastic with life as I was. Alone in the corner of the supermarket car park, I heaved the bin bag of clothes Richard had left behind from the boot of my car and dropped it into the charity bin, dusting off my hands as though that meant he was out of my life for good. It was then that my attention was drawn to a cardboard box sitting amongst the puddles, almost buried beneath a mountain of recycling encircling the glass bottle bank. Rats, I thought as it shuffled and I backed away but then, quite unmistakably, the box meowed. Frowning I pushed aside the rubbish, lifted the box lid and found myself nose to nose with five kittens. One was white, another grey, two were cinnamon coloured and the last was a spotty mix of everything. They looked up at me unsure and afraid, and I stared back, already falling in love all over again.

Less than two months later I opened the cards on my twenty-ninth birthday to find that there was a cat on the front of all but one. I smiled and stood them in a line along the kitchen table then took another sip of coffee and looked over at my laptop as it made a number of irritated beeps. Bea was standing on the keyboard, her tail held high as she looked back at me with large innocent eyes. But innocent she most certainly was not. Of all the kittens I'd acquired that May day there had been only one boy. Modi I'd called him and like Bea, he was predominantly cinnamon coloured. He was also well mannered and hassle-free, two things his sister was not. Although the runt of the litter, what Bea lacked in size she made up for in spirit and once she realised I was eating toast she made a dash for my knee, knocking over the birthday cards on her way. I didn't put up much of a fight and broke her off a small piece, then I stood the cards back up trying not to notice that I was two shy from last year. Sophie had been my best friend for years and bridesmaid at my wedding. Richard had once promised that this year I'd spend my birthday in Venice, but as I sat alone at the kitchen table I couldn't help but wonder if right now the two of them were there together. I shook my head, telling myself not to think about such things, and surrendered the rest of my toast to Bea. It was time to go to work.

My cottage sat on the outskirts of a small village perched on the edge of the Peak District, surrounded by grassy hills and dry stone walls. The day looked warm beyond the French blue painted windows and I called,

'See you later guys,' as I picked up the car keys and opened my front door. 'Be good,' I smiled as five pairs of eyes looked back at me from various vantage points of the kitchen.

I walked towards the gate, an azure blue sky overhead, and then climbed into my rumbly old Citroen CV, the roads still quiet as I headed into town.

Squeezed in between a florists and Harper's Bookshop on the main street, Brambly Antiques had an elegant black shop front with gold lettering and two storeys of red brick above. Inside, the exposed beams were lime washed white, the terracotta floor blanketed in Persian rugs and the room abundant with treasures from throughout the ages. Ramblers and tourists were already strolling down the town's cobbled streets as I opened up the shop and suddenly I felt hungry to get stuck into some work.

'Hi Harriet, sorry I'm late.'

'No trouble,' I said as Charlie arrived ten minutes later and shrugged off her jacket. Charlie had olive skin and dark hair and at twenty-three, had been working for me for almost twelve months.

'Lovely day isn't it? And of course, happy birthday!' Charlie pulled a purple envelope from her bag followed by a small box.

'How cute!' I said, this time faced with a litter of kittens as I opened the card. Inside the box was a pair of cat silhouette shaped earrings and I smiled. 'Thank you.'

Charlie was the sort of girl who loved buying gifts and looked pleased with my response. I stood the card on the counter and she asked, 'Up to anything special tonight?'

'I'm cooking dinner for my family.'

'All of them?' She looked impressed. 'That's quite a gathering.'

'I'm looking forward to it,' I smiled. 'There's a lot of catching up to do.' Having hammered in a nail, I picked up a painting and hung it on the wall, squinting as I nudged it straight.

'So where did you nip off to last night?'

I stiffened, surprised Charlie had guessed that anything had been up. 'Nowhere special, dentist appointment,' I spluttered, my gaze lingering unnecessarily on the painting. The last thing I was going to tell her was the truth. I'd only agreed to go on the date to stop Lou nagging. The phone rang and I dashed perhaps a little too eagerly towards it. 'Brambly Antiques, how can I help you?'

'Sis' hey, it's Ryan. Happy birthday!'

'Thanks, how are things?'

'Well, I'm ringing because Karen can't come tonight.'

'Oh what's up? You know you can just say if she hates my cooking.'

Ryan laughed. 'No, she's feeling rough. She's got a cold, lost her voice, the works.'

It was common knowledge that Karen didn't get on with her husband's side of the family, with the exception of my mum, and I wondered whether she really was so conveniently unwell or not. Either way I wished her my best and told my brother I looked forward to seeing him later.

'I'm just going upstairs Charlie,' I called as I headed for the wooden staircase in the corner of the room. I was trying to avoid further interrogation and Charlie knew it. 'You okay with everything down here?'

'Sure,' she said.

8

The treads creaked underfoot as I bypassed the first floor full of more antiquarian curiosities and climbed to the second. My workshop was light and airy compared to the rooms below but as usual it was a mess. I could already hear voices downstairs as I walked over to the sash windows and heaved them open, welcoming the sunshine in, and for a minute I gazed down at the street below and then glanced over the rooftops of the buildings opposite, just able to glimpse the turrets of the castle on the other side of town. I'd known the view since I was a child, when the workshop belonged to my father.

Turning back to the room I looked at the mound of newly acquired stock stacked in the corner. Every weekend I went to local flea markets and car boots, on the hunt for unique treasures that people were throwing out, unable to see their potential as I did, and I rarely went away empty handed. Last Sunday had been no exception and amongst the goods I'd returned with were old baskets, copper pans, books and silverware. I crouched and lifted the lid of a vintage trunk, surveying the damage that years of neglect had inflicted. It had to be late nineteenth century and I frowned as I caught sight of a label stuck inside the lid and tried to read the handwriting. It had once belonged to a Madame Jeanne Hecquet from Paris and I pondered how it was that it had come to be in the middle of England. A little tender loving care would be required before the trunk was ready for the shop but I had seen worse.

Beside it sat a heap of enamelware and I picked up the nearest pitcher. It was a little rusty and chipped in places but once the dust was wiped away I knew it would look charming downstairs, perhaps displayed with some flowers in. My gaze then ran over a copper

9

kettle and the ornate frame of a mirror before stopping on a painting. I leant forwards and picked it up. It was a landscape, the sky moody above a large majestic lake, and my eyes wandered over the surface of the canvas as I remembered the last time I had visited the Lake District. I'd been to many countries and places but nowhere for me had matched it. Richard had always been disparaging, unable to see what I did. To him it was just the place where he had grown up, nothing more, but if there was one thing I thanked him for, it was introducing us. The painting was shrouded in a crude frame and the glass was ill-fitting, but its housing for the past goodness knows how many years had at least kept it safe. I took it back to my desk and propped it up against the wall. Then I reached for a bottle of cleaner and a heavy copper pan.

By the time Charlie took her lunch break I had polished a set of six copper pans and a whole host of silver flatware, and I carried them downstairs where I set them down on a table. An elderly woman was deliberating over a coffer across the room, whispering with her friend, and having returned to the counter with a handful of books which needed pricing, I looked towards the door as it was pushed open. The man who walked in was tall and blonde, a few years older than myself with a smile that made me wish he had been sitting opposite me last night. Slowly he began to peruse the room and I looked back down at the book, but before I had chance to jot the price inside the cover he was standing in front of me.

'Hi,' he said. He was even better looking up close.

'Hi,' I repeated.

'The tapestry hanging up behind you; is it French?'

'Flemish,' I said. 'Fifteenth century.'

He wanted a closer look and before I could say *personal space* he had skirted around the counter and was standing next to me. I subtly shuffled backwards until I felt something behind my knees.

'It depicts the Sybil of Cumae,' I offered. 'Here, you see?'

'Yes, yes,' he murmured, looking across at me with another smile and he only looked away after I did first and immediately I wished I hadn't. I started reeling off some other facts, not to sound smart but to fill the slender gap between us with something other than an awkward silence, completely unaware that the woman interested in the coffer had crossed the room and was trying to get my attention.

'Excuse me?' she tried again in a meek voice.

This time I heard her and as I span back to the room my fingertips brushed the man's thigh. I couldn't believe it. I felt like such a clumsy fool and I didn't need a mirror to know that I had instantly turned an unattractive shade of crimson. I clenched my fingers into fists, and biting my bottom lip I looked back at him.

'I'm so sorry,' I spluttered.

He didn't say anything but it was clear from his expression that he was amused. I asked the ground to swallow me up but as the seconds on the grandfather clock ticked loudly by in the otherwise silent room, it seemed I'd have to make it out of there on my own. I looked down, my face screwed up in agony and at last sidled out from behind the counter.

'How can I help you?' I asked the elderly woman, trying to keep my voice level. She had all the characteristics of a mouse, from her rounded shoulders to the small hands which clutched her handbag tightly.

She opened her mouth to speak but it was her friend beyond her shoulder who answered first.

'We'd like to know your best price on this?' she said curtly, her voice masculine and her expression stern.

She was the shape of a diamond but lacked the elegance of one and when I gave my answer she rebuffed it with a snort.

'I don't think so Julie, not for that.'

Julie glanced from me to the coffer and then back at her companion with fidgety lips as though she wanted to speak but daren't. I could see it in her eyes that she wanted to say yes but her friend was already walking away, directing her towards another chest that was far inferior in quality and was reflected so in the price tag. 'This one's much better,' she stated confidently.

Julie knew she was obliged to follow but didn't.

'It's a lovely piece,' I smiled, leading her back to the original coffer in question. 'It's made of oak and the craftsmanship is superb.' I lifted the lid so that she could look inside and I watched as she gently ran her fingers over the dark wood. 'It's likely Elizabethan as you can tell from-'

'It's not as nice as this one,' Julie's friend interrupted as though determined she would be the one to decide.

Julie pulled back her hand like a child whose fingers had been caught in the biscuit tin and like a spurned hound, she peered over her shoulder before loyally, albeit with great reluctance, thanked me for my assistance and caught up with her companion.

I closed the coffer lid, unsure whether to be amused by the pair or not, and then sensed that someone was standing behind me.

'I'll take it,' the blonde guy said as I turned around. 'Could you hold it until next week?'

'Sure,' I said.

He left a deposit and a smile and when the doorbell rang again it was Charlie returning from her lunch break.

'Hello, I'm back,' she called but then stopped in her tracks as she saw me perched on the bottom tread of the staircase, lost in my thoughts. 'Are you all right?' she frowned.

'Yes, I'm fine,' I lied as I stood back up and walked over to the counter and the books that still needed pricing. I knew she didn't believe me. I was a bad liar but I was incapable of putting what I felt into words even if I had the courage to talk about it out loud.

'What's happened?'

'Nothing,' I said, offering her the most convincing smile I could muster. 'The tapestry's sold by the way. A man's coming back next week for it.'

When I got home I could see Modi lounging in the garden, soaking up the late afternoon sunshine, and I knew the others wouldn't be far away. I unlatched the gate and suddenly they appeared, dashing towards me like I was the pied piper playing their favourite tune. I appreciated the greeting.

'It's good to see you too girls.'

Flicks was a meek white cat and loved to sleep in the most unusual of places. From the looks of her fur, speckled with compost, the wheelbarrow was currently her favourite spot to kip. Coco had undoubtedly spent the afternoon playing in the garden shed amongst the stacks of plant pots if her cobweb covered head was anything to go by. She was an adventurous sort and her fur a spotty mishmash of browns, white and ginger, almost as though she were wearing camouflage face paint. Then there was Mona, named so because she loved her food and didn't stop moaning until she got it. She had a beautiful long grey coat and dewy eyes that never failed to win me over. Bea was hungry too but as usual one step ahead of everyone else, including me. I heard the shopping bag at my feet fall over and then saw, not to my surprise, her ginger tail poking out of it.

'Hold on there you,' I said, persuading her out and then picking the bag back up. 'We're not inside yet.'

Modi was still climbing to his feet, stretching as though he'd been in that spot amongst the geranium's all afternoon, but by the time I unlocked the front door he'd caught us up. Excitably they circled my feet as we crossed the kitchen, their trust in me outweighing any fear of being trodden on, and then once I'd filled their bowls I continued on into the living room alone.

Having dropped into my chair I listened to the silence and my gaze bore into the vacant chair across from me until tears blurred it into obscurity. Richard had been there, in the back of my mind all day. Like every day. No matter how hard I tried I missed him. I was supposed to hate him after what he'd done but still I closed my eyes wanting to hear his voice. If I tried hard enough I almost could. I pretended I could feel his breath on my face, his hand in my hair, unable to imagine replacing him with someone else as he had done me. With a deep shaky breath I wiped the moisture from my face with the back of my hand and then opening my eyes felt, against all the odds, a spark of amusement lighten my load. Suddenly sitting in Richard's chair and looking back at me, was Modi. I got up, walked over to the chair and sat down on the carpet then reached out with my fingertips and stroked his head, smiling as he nuzzled back into my hand. His fur was so smooth and as his chest slowly rose and fell beneath my hand and he looked back at me with large yellow eyes which seemed to gaze deeper than the surface, I felt a surge of love for him which had beaten back my tears more than once before.

'What would I do without you?' I said as he reached out towards my face with a paw as though trying to dry my cheeks.

Modi gave me strength at times like this like no person could and I knew that as long as he was there, I'd be okay. He was the man of the house now and I just hoped that unlike his predecessor, he would never abandon me.

'Happy birthday!'

'Wow!' My eyes widened as I looked at the cake my sister was holding, a large twenty-nine blaring more boldly than I felt from the iced summit. 'Thank you,' I said, retreating into the kitchen and welcoming Lou and her fiancé Tom indoors. 'Drink?'

'Oh yes,' Lou replied, finding a space to slide the cake onto the counter. 'Wine for me.'

My little sister had large green eyes and disciplined blonde hair that, as always, framed her face perfectly. Her dress was elegant but not over the top, her legs long and toned and suddenly I felt as though I'd gained twenty pounds, got dressed in a train toilet cubicle and completely forgotten to do my hair. I didn't miss that her clutch matched Tom's shirt either.

'I'll have a beer,' he said.

Lou looked around and smiled. 'It smells great in here.'

'The others are in the living room,' I said as I gave them their drinks and then tucked my loose blonde curls behind my ears.

There was another knock on the door. 'Happy birthday Harriet.'

'Last but not least,' I smiled as I hugged my youngest brother. 'It's been way too long.'

'You look nice,' he said.

'Thanks. You look great yourself!' Ollie had a Mohican but that evening left it down so that his blonde hair fell limp across his left eye. His stubble was a couple of days old and he wore a leather jacket and jeans. 'How are you?' I asked.

'Good,' he nodded. 'The train was hectic but I made it in one piece.'

'I would have picked you up from the station you know?' I said, smiling.

'It's okay, I knew you'd be busy.'

'You want something to drink? Beer?'

'Yes thanks.'

I opened the fridge as laughter erupted from the living room which was by then very full and uncharacteristically bustling, chairs and stools fetched from all over to accommodate for everyone.

'We've all been looking forward to seeing you,' I said as I turned back to him. 'Shall we go through?'

'After you birthday girl,' he said.

'Ollie! Hey,' my eldest brother cried as we walked through the door. His name was Will and he worked in advertising which is where he'd met Mel, the latest in his string of girlfriends. Then there was my brother Ryan, an architect and as I'd been told to expect, no Karen. Lou was a textile designer and had been engaged to Tom since New Year's. My younger brother Chris was a journalist and had just moved in with his girlfriend Emily, and then, in the midst of their grown offspring were my parents.

Ollie was the youngest of us all and for him, music was his life. Since his band had been signed six months ago he'd barely seen any of us and as he was greeted with hugs and slaps on the back, I tried to remember the last time we had all been together in the same room. Out of the six of us, I was the only one who had not left the area where we had been raised and so occasions such as these were few and far between. Then I realised it had been the day I'd married Richard.

'To you Harriet!' Suddenly everyone was staring at me, their drinks held aloft. 'Happy birthday!' my dad said.

I smiled appreciatively, sipped my wine and waited for the talking to resume before I slipped off to the kitchen. *Pull yourself together*, I told myself angrily and then sighed as I knocked a spoon onto the floor. Bending down to pick it up I only then noticed that the four legged members of my large family were hiding under the table and the creases fell out of my brow.

'Don't be scared,' I whispered. They weren't used to so many people.

'So?'

Startled, I glanced up to find that Lou was standing in the doorway. I didn't think she'd waste much time in cornering me but still I hadn't expected her onslaught of questions just yet, and from the look on her face she was getting straight to the point.

'You didn't return my call last night,' she said. 'How did it go? What did you think of him?'

I stood back up and grabbed an oven mitt. 'Nice, I guess.'

'Nice?' Lou sounded less than impressed with me.

'He just-'

'Wasn't Richard,' she interrupted and heaving a sigh I turned away from her. 'For God's sake Harriet, you can't just keep collecting cats until you've matched Richard's body mass in fur and whiskers, although admittedly you're about there.'

Lou was always quick to get bullish and I wished she'd drop the subject. 'That's not what I'm doing,' I said, my brow creasing, and then Modi crept out from under the table and rubbed against my ankle. 'Though they do help,' I added quietly.

'What helps,' she said, 'is getting back out there. Meet new guys.'

How did she know, I thought. How did she know how it felt to wake up in an empty bed, my husband gone and nothing but a letter left to explain it all? Just a letter; as though I deserved nothing more. But, as usual, I didn't say anything out loud. I knew she wouldn't listen. I'd lose the debate as soon as start it so instead I nodded dutifully and murmured some sort of agreement then went to take the cottage pie out of the oven whether the top was golden brown yet or not. A room full of hungry guests waiting next door was as good an excuse as any to head for the exit.

'I just want you to be happy,' she said, her hand falling on my arm. 'You know that right?'

I forced myself to look at her and knew she meant it. 'I know.'

She smiled and then realising Modi was at my feet abruptly she bent down and picked him up. 'I tell you what though, he'd make a cracking pair of gloves.'

Modi started to squirm and Lou frowned, confused why he'd want to escape.

'Hey, I didn't mean it,' she frowned and then she let out a little scream as he at last wriggled free and ran from the kitchen. 'He scratched me,' she said. 'Look at that,' she insisted, showing me a minute mark on the back of her hand.

I looked and made the right noises to imply my sympathy but couldn't deny that behind the facade I was hiding a small smile.

'Anything I can do to help?' my mum asked, at that moment appearing in the doorway.

'Perfect timing,' I replied. 'Let's eat.'

'Sorry it's a bit tight,' I apologised once we'd pushed some tables together in the living room and everyone began to squeeze round.

'If there's one thing we're good at, it's sharing,' my dad smiled, shuffling along to his seat. 'We've had to do it enough over the years.'

He was right; we'd grown up in a small three bedroom cottage with no back garden. Now elbow to elbow around the table once more I was reminded of those days, and judging from the conversation as we ate, I wasn't the only one.

When it came to the cake I blew out the candles of which, to my insistence, we were several short and once we could eat no more I was bombarded with gifts. Looking at the assortment of strangely shaped packages in front of me I could already see a certain theme running through them all. If the paper wasn't covered in cats it was paw patterned and I soon discovered that what waited inside was little different. There was a cat shaped mug; an apron with a cat on the front; a cat decorated laptop bag; a cat tablecloth; cat stationary; and some chocolate mice. Lou's smile was the broadest of all as I unwrapped a pair of knickers stamped with *crazy cat lady* on the bum.

'I couldn't resist,' she grinned.

I smiled along with everyone else but couldn't deny that deep down inside something was niggling at me. What had happened, I asked myself. Not that long ago I hadn't even considered having a cat, never mind five. In fact until I found that small needy family I hadn't had an animal in my life. Venturing into the pet aisle for the first time had felt as foreign as finding my way round the plumbing section when there had been a leak under the kitchen sink, and yet it was official; I had become The Crazy Cat Lady of the family. But I wasn't a slightly insane old woman dressed in fur covered cardigans that watched cat videos on YouTube. I didn't hold the record for singlehandedly clearing the shop shelves of tinned tuna in thirty seconds flat and as yet I hadn't put them all in a pram and taken them for a walk as though they were the children I didn't have.

But I'd found five abandoned kittens, taken them in, and for it I'd been branded. I wondered whether I should speak up. Should I argue my case before it was too late? But it was like being declared insane, anything I said disregarded and simply considered only further evidence of my condition.

'Karen's been pestering for a cat,' Ryan commented, breaking my train of thought. 'I don't suppose you have one spare do you Harriet?'

'I'd love one too,' Mel added, looking sideways at Chris as though it had long been a point of contention.

I looked back down at the gifts I'd received and realised that this was my last chance. I could still turn back if I really wanted. I could give them all away, pass off the title and indeed put it down to a brief spell of insanity.

But at that moment I saw Bea peep her nose around

the corner of the door and smiled. That day, when we'd first met, that box of kittens had rescued me as much as I had rescued them. The rest of the world didn't have to understand. What did it matter what they thought or said? If I was honest I no longer had a choice, it had been made two months ago, and so despite any doubts my answer to Ryan's question was no.

TWO

'Morning Mrs Ellis,' I smiled from my front garden.

My austere faced neighbour did not smile back, as indeed I had expected.

'Hello Miss Hunt,' she replied, her tone disapproving as though she was a teacher and I a troublesome pupil.

At first I used to wonder what it was about me Mrs Ellis disliked so much but I'd since learnt that she had a quarrel with the entire world. With a bovine-like strut and a physique to match, I wondered if Mrs Ellis had ever been a catch. Considering what a gentleman Mr Ellis was, I presumed so.

'Hello Harriet,' he said as he appeared in toe and followed his wife down the garden path.

'Hello Eddie,' I called. As usual he had a walking stick in one hand but strolled towards the gate more like the lead in a musical than a man in his seventies.

'Open the car,' Mrs Ellis barked impatiently as Eddie stalled to point out a goldfinch sitting on the bird table.

'Coming dear.'

He sung it more than said it and I watched with a small smile as his wife tore open the car door and climbed into the passenger seat.

'Wow, she's as fierce as a bulldog.'

I spun round and saw Ollie was standing in the doorway with a mug of coffee in his hand.

'You're right there,' I replied, grinning. 'You sleep okay?'

'Like a log,' he said as he peeled himself off the door frame and then wandered towards the outdoor table and dropped into one of the chairs.

I turned away from the recycling bin now full of empty wine and beer bottles, and joined him. The garden smelt of roses and the blue sky was criss-crossed with aeroplane tracks.

'Did you enjoy yourself last night?' he asked.

I nodded. 'And I'm glad you could make it. I heard your new song on the radio yesterday by the way,' I said. 'I almost forgot to tell you.'

'What do you think?'

'It's your best yet. Charlie loves it too.' I frowned then added, 'I'm not sure she believes you're my brother though.'

Ollie laughed and then out of nowhere Modi jumped onto his lap.

'I'm sorry,' I said as Modi nestled down, purring nosily like he'd found the best seat in the house. 'He likes attention. You can push him off if you want.'

'It's all right,' Ollie said. He ran a hand over Modi's ginger fur. 'Everyone needs a bit of attention every now and then.' Modi continued to purr and then both Ollie's expression and tone changed. 'I'm sorry about you and Rich, Harriet.'

I shied away from my brother's gaze and looked at Modi as he lifted his head, Ollie complying to tickle him under the chin.

'He'd been seeing her for more than a month,' I said and it hurt in the back of my throat as though each word had been dragged out by barbed wire. I waited for the pain to ease and Ollie didn't push me. 'Sometimes I feel foolish,' I said when I could carry on, 'as though I should have known.'

'You thought he was a good guy,' Ollie said, shaking his head. 'We all did.'

'Perhaps I should have been more like Mrs Ellis,' I joked, spluttering a small laugh. 'She's doing something right to have been married forty years.'

'Or perhaps it was Richard who was in the wrong,' Ollie replied and I detected anger in his voice. Suddenly his fists were clenched but Modi didn't seem to have noticed that the fussing had stopped.

'What would you have done?' I asked. 'If you had been me?'

Ollie took a moment to think. 'Written a song about it,' he eventually said, a small smile breaking the tension in his face.

'Good answer,' I nodded, finding a smile too.

It felt good not to be alone. The house had become very quiet since the day Richard had left and my brother's company was a pleasant respite to the silence at breakfast. Swallows were dashing in circles overhead and then returning to their nests for hungry chicks tucked underneath the roofline of the house. Soon it would be time for them to leave its safety and venture ahead alone. Ollie had dared to do just that, my other siblings too, but lingering in the back of my mind was the fear that perhaps I had been left behind, too afraid

24

to spread my wings in case I fell. The nest in which I'd grown up had always been very full but last night I had been reminded of how empty it had become. My siblings had moved on. Their lives were exciting and bright. In the past I had been more than happy with what I had, never worried about my future. I'd known that it was a path I wouldn't be walking alone and with Richard beside me I'd be happy. He was all I really needed after all. But now that life was in tatters and if I didn't have him then what did I have?

I didn't realise I'd been nibbling my thumb nail until it started hurting and grimacing I clenched my fist. I looked back at my house and remembered the day Richard and I had first stood in front of the door. Together we had turned it into a home, every corner of every room, but now I was trying to eradicate each last piece of him from it and although his belongings were gone, the memories would never fade.

I looked across at Ollie as he placed his hand on mine. 'Let's go for a walk,' he suggested. 'It feels a lifetime since I last felt grass beneath my feet.'

A gentle breeze tugged at my hair and as I looked down the muddy track ahead, towards the stile at the end, I tucked what I could behind my ear.

'What?' Ollie said as I fought with a grin, but he already knew why I was smiling.

On our way through the village we had been stopped by two teenage girls, their eyes wide and cheeks red as they recognised the drummer from their favourite band. Giggling excitably, they'd asked him to sign their t-shirts and then if they could have their picture taken with him.

'If they find out where I live I'll never get rid of

them,' I told him.

He laughed but I spotted a glimmer of self-consciousness in his expression.

We reached the stile and I climbed over, stepping down ankle deep into a field of dandelions.

'I remember coming here when we were young,' Ollie said and he grabbed a head of grass and pulled off the seed.

'I remember too,' I replied.

'You always had that sketch book tucked under your arm.'

I remembered that as well.

'Do you still draw?' he asked.

I shook my head. 'No.' He didn't ask why but I found myself reeling off excuses, unsure which, or indeed if any, were true.

'I liked your portraits the most,' Ollie said. 'I still have that one you drew of me.'

'You do?' I replied, incredulous.

He nodded. 'Of course.'

Cattle were grazing at the far end of the field and as we approached them they lifted their heads, still chomping at an easy, relaxed pace. We walked across the fields until our legs ached, our path and our conversation both reminiscent of our childhood, but I knew that Ollie would soon be leaving and my smile along with him. He had a train to catch at four and I found myself counting down the hours as much as I tried not to.

'I'll make us some lunch,' I said to Ollie when we got back.

'Okay, thanks,' he smiled and then his phone rang. A frown settled across his face when he answered it and he walked outside into the garden. Although his words were muffled through the kitchen window I could tell that whoever he was speaking to didn't have good news.

'Everything okay?' I asked when I brought out something to eat and found him sitting quietly with Modi once again on his knee.

Ollie didn't say yes, just told me that he was fine, and I knew his answer was only to appease me.

'You sure?' I said, handing him a drink. 'You know I'm a good listener.'

Ollie looked down and put a hand through his hair and when he lifted his head again I thought for a moment he might tell me.

'No, honestly, it's fine,' he said with a shrug of the shoulders. 'I wouldn't want to bore you.'

'I don't think you would bore me,' I replied but still he didn't open up and I knew not to push him any further. He wasn't a little boy anymore as much as I wanted to still look out for him. He would tell me if and when he was ready, and when that time came he knew where to find me.

Ollie put down his bag and turned back to face me. His train would be here any minute.

'It was really good to see you,' I smiled.

'Yeah it's been good,' he said. 'I'm sorry I have to leave so soon.'

'I understand, you're busy,' I told him but my heart felt heavy and I wished he wasn't going yet.

He smiled and was about to say something when the loud speaker interrupted, echoing loudly around the station.

'Here it is,' he said as the train rumbled into the platform.

I crossed my arms as a gust of wind that came with it hit us like a wall.

'Don't forget about me will you?' I asked.

He looked at me, his eyes warm, and then he held me in his arms.

'I'll be back as soon as I can,' he said over my shoulder. 'Take care, okay?'

I subtly wiped away a tear as he picked up his bag. 'You too,' I smiled.

He gave one last small nod and then he turned away and boarded the train, and my footsteps ran along the platform parallel with his walking down the aisle until he found an empty seat. He mouthed a last goodbye through the glass and then the train was again on its way.

The breeze was picking up as I walked back to my car. I'd been undecided whether to call in at a nearby flea market before heading back home but turning the ignition I felt far from in the mood. Instead I diverted to the supermarket for some essentials before leaving town; Saturday night had almost wiped me out. A basket in one hand I strode with purpose down the aisles, reaching out for the usual suspects that filled my kitchen cupboards without any desire to try something new. The sooner I got home the longer I could spend in the garden and it desperately needed some attention.

'Harriet? Is that you?'

I turned around to face the woman with a short dark bob already dreading the conversation which lay unavoidably ahead. 'Sian,' I smiled meekly. 'How are you?'

'I'm fantastic!' she beamed. 'You? Oh how rude of me, this is Steven, my fiancé.' She grabbed the arm of the man beside her. 'Steven, this is Harriet, the one I was telling you about with loads of cats.'

I wanted to tell Sian that the next time she asked a question, it was polite to wait for the response whether she was bothered about hearing how I was or not. As for her introduction, I still wasn't sure I'd heard correctly. It seemed I wasn't the 'old friend' or 'woman with the antique shop', but 'the weird one with lots of cats'.

'Nice to meet you,' I said, finding my voice.

'Yeah, hiya,' Steven said with a slight inclination of the head, his hands buried in his pockets.

Sian clung to him as though afraid if she let go he would drift away. I had known her since the age of three when my favourite teddy bear and I would be invited round at weekends to play. We pretended to drink tea from plastic cups and saucers and when we grew out of make believe dinner parties, Sian would borrow her mum's make-up bag. As teenagers we had shared secrets and giggled about boys but beyond high school we had grown apart, leaving us with nothing but mutual friends and memories in common. The last I'd heard she was working as a receptionist and had got engaged again, and this time I hadn't been invited to the party.

'So how are they?' she asked, her eyes wide.

'Who?' I frowned.

'Your cats, of course,' she replied giggling. She peered into the basket slung over my forearm as though counting the tins of meat.

'Fine,' I said flatly. I knew Sian didn't care and years of experience warned me that I was being mocked.

'I've been meaning to call you actually,' she said. 'After...well that palaver with...with you know?'

I wasn't sure what to say to that other than if she had wanted to call she would have done so two months ago, and so I said nothing.

'Hey we should go out for drinks one night!' Sian abruptly cried.

That was the last thing I needed but I knew it would never materialise and so didn't argue.

'Great,' she beamed, touching my hand once again in the hope that I might at last comment on her ring.

'I'm just going to carry on,' Steven interrupted, wriggling from Sian's vice. 'Catch me up? Nice to meet you Harriet.'

As he walked away Sian stuck out her bottom lip, clearly irritated, but then remembered I was there and tucked it back in. 'We're going to Venice in August,' she blurted.

That was the first knock to hit home. 'I've heard it's amazing,' I stumbled.

'It was either there or Paris,' she told me, 'but I decided Venice was probably more romantic.'

'Yes, good choice,' I murmured.

'Are you going away anywhere this summer?'

I moved my weight from one foot to the other. 'No, I don't have any plans.'

Suddenly her expression crumpled with pity. 'Yes of course.'

I assumed by that she meant that being single why would I. I looked down at my feet as a fresh wave of melancholia washed over me.

'Well I've got to go,' she suddenly said with a smile that was brighter than necessary. 'It was lovely seeing you again.'

'You too,' I said but the smile was strained and it quickly faded as she walked away.

*

I put my hands in the kitchen sink and watched as the clear water turned brown. It was dark outside and it was only the lack of light which had at last persuaded me to put down the garden trowel and finish for the evening. A blister at the top of my palm was hurting but I ignored it and continued washing the dirt off my fingers. I looked out of the window in front of me; a star stood alone against a deep blue sky, the first to appear that night. I looked back at my hands, earth still caught behind my nails, but I tipped away the water and then half-filled a vase from the tap. A bunch of roses lay on the kitchen table and I breathed in their scent before placing them one by one into the vase. I looked down as Flicks rubbed against my ankle.

'What do you think?' I asked her as I perfected the arrangement. She looked back up at me with that serious expression of hers and then squeaked a tender meow.

I walked into the living room with Flicks on my tail and placed the vase on an antique side table. It was a recent addition to the room which I'd found at a car boot and it perfectly filled the gap where Richard's guitar had once sat, and hid the indentation that the ever inanimate instrument had made in the carpet.

Sian's 'of course' comment had haunted the rest of my afternoon, greedily gnawing away at my attention as determined as the weeds I was pulling out of the earth, but as my energy burnt away so did the rawness of the injury. For the first time I began to feel the chill of the evening and picked up a jumper slung over the back of a nearby chair, then pulled it over my head.

As my eyes fell on the bookcase across the room I

remembered what Ollie had said about my drawing and reached up for my old sketch book on the top shelf. It was covered in a layer of dust and for the first time since I'd hidden it up there, the spine creaked as I opened the cover. There had been a time when I always had the book to hand and charcoal stained my fingers. I flicked through the pages remembering the landscapes and faces I'd drawn with a small smile, hesitating longest on a sketch of Richard not long after we'd first met. The next page was blank, and all those after it. It appeared that my heart, which had once been in my work, had been stolen back then but if Richard had since gone and it wasn't in the sketch book, then to whom did it now belong?

At that moment a pair of white ears appeared from behind the sketch book, followed by a pink nose. Flicks had climbed onto the back of my armchair and was wavering on her two back legs as she reached out towards me.

'Yes, I think you're right Flicks,' I said, putting the book aside and then whisking her up in my arms. 'It belongs to the five of you.'

THREE

I woke up Monday morning with a headache, unaware at that point that the day had no intention of improving from there. Feeling hazy I pulled myself out of bed and then stumped my toe on the way to the bathroom, hopping and cursing the rest of the way. After close inspection I decided that the toe was salvageable but then frowned as I caught sight of my reflection in the mirror over the sink. My hair indisputably resembled a hawthorn thicket and I reached for the hairbrush with little expectation that something agreeable could be made of it. In the end it was thrust into a bun and I headed for the stairs feeling as ready as I ever would to meet the day.

'Yes Mona, I'll be right there,' I assured the greediest of my cats as I put some bread in the toaster and then rushed to answer the phone.

'Hello? Hello? Damn cold callers,' I muttered as I returned to the kitchen and that was when I heard the first drops of rain hit the window. I looked out into the garden and then the heavy grey sky above it. 'Great,' I sighed. It hadn't only been the flowers who'd appreciated the sunshine lately.

'Here you go fellas,' I said as I poured out five bowls of biscuits but then noticed I was one diner short. 'Modi? Modi where are you?' I strode through to the living room but he wasn't in there either. 'Damn,' I cried, having forgotten about my own breakfast and I dashed back to the kitchen to find that it smelt of burnt toast.

When the time came to take off for work Modi still hadn't shown up but telling myself that he was likely just sleeping under a hedge and was fine, I got in the car and drove to town.

It was a quiet morning, the drizzle dissuading the shoppers from their homes, and by lunch that drizzle had turned into a downpour. Staring out of the window I watched it lash against the glass and then shook myself free of my reverie as I heard Charlie call me.

'What was that?' I asked, turning back to the shop.

Charlie was standing there with two mugs. 'Coffee?' she said. 'While we've got a minute.'

'Thanks,' I smiled as I wrapped my hands around the warmth of the cup and sat down. 'Did you have a good weekend?'

Charlie nodded and a smile flickered across her face. 'The best.'

Something was different about her today. She'd been cheerier than I'd ever known all morning and as she put down her coffee, I sensed she was prepping to spill the beans.

'What is it Charlie?' Now I was smiling too, riddled with curiosity.

She leant forwards and took a deep breath. 'I'm

going to be a mum.'

That was not what I had expected. Engaged perhaps, but not pregnant and somehow my heart was filled with joy and yet dashed of it at the same time. I'd always had visions of being a mum someday but it was something to look forward to in the future. I'd always been too busy with work and if I was honest I hadn't been ready for it. But then I'd found that the future was suddenly my present and the man I'd loved had walked away without looking back. Suddenly my chances looked bleak. What if it happened again? What if I didn't find anyone at all? I swallowed my fears, unable to digest them yet but persuading them out of the way in order to find a smile.

'I'm so happy for you,' I said, placing my hand on hers. 'You must be so excited.'

Charlie laughed as though unable to contain it any longer. 'Yes, we are.'

I took another sip of coffee and listened as Charlie told me how she couldn't stop smiling. I remembered the feeling but it had been a long time since such a smile had crept across my face for no other reason than I was so happy.

'Are you hoping for a boy or a girl?' I asked.

'Honestly I don't mind,' Charlie said. 'And Greg's already started looking for a bigger place. He says we can hardly stay where we are.'

'I'm jealous,' I admitted. 'Does this mean I'm going to have to find a new assistant?'

Charlie laughed again. 'I'm not going anywhere just yet.'

I told Charlie to get her lunch and once she had disappeared into the office I snatched up a rag and a bottle of window cleaner. Whenever the path ahead was blurry it always seemed to me that cleaning the windows was a good start towards untangling it all. I vigorously wiped the glass as the rain continued to shower it from the other side and I only stopped when I heard the doorbell ring. As my aching arm dropped to my side I saw that it was the man who had reserved the tapestry.

'An unusual day to clean the windows,' he said with a grin once he had closed the door on the wild weather.

'I was in the mood,' I replied as I stepped off the hop-up I'd been using to reach the parameters of the window.

'I'd go for a jog if I were you.'

'Excuse me?' I frowned, wondering what he was commenting on.

'When I'm brassed off I go for a jog,' he explained. 'Although not in this weather I grant you. It helps me cool off.'

'Oh,' I smiled. 'Is it that obvious?' I asked as I walked back to the counter and put down the rag and bottle.

He shrugged. 'I'm right aren't I?'

I didn't attest to the contrary.

'I'm Sean by the way.'

'And you're here for the tapestry,' I said.

'Yes.' He was still smiling and only then did he look at the tapestry.

'It's one of the best I've ever come across,' I told him, turning to look at it as well.

'Me too,' he replied. 'Although it were your sale tactics which I couldn't refuse.'

I glanced back at him feeling my cheeks burn again, the intensity of his attention flattering but making me uncomfortable.

He picked one of my business cards off the counter. 'Would you mind if I took one of these?'

'Of course not,' I smiled.

'Harriet Hunt,' he read aloud and then slipped it into his jean's pocket. 'You have a pleasant shop here.'

'Thank you.'

'Have you been here many years?' he asked.

'The shop, yes,' I replied. 'It's a family business but I only took over from my father three years ago.'

'Your father?' he repeated.

'Yes, Henry.'

'Hunt?'

'That's right.'

'So you're not married?' he asked.

I shook my head and trying not to blush said, 'No.'

'But you have a boyfriend?'

'No,' I said again.

He frowned but the corners of his mouth still curled upwards. 'I'm not sure I believe you.'

'Trust me, it's not something a girl lies about.'

He paused for a moment. 'In that case would you go for a drink with me?'

Before I could answer the doorbell rang again and a woman with blonde hair and stilettoes shook her umbrella and then brushed the hair from her face with blood red nails.

'Hello,' she said brightly and Sean took a speedy step back. 'Oh wow!' Her eyes lit up as she caught sight of the tapestry and joining us, she slipped an arm around Sean's. 'It's beautiful.'

Caught up in my confusion, it took me longer than usual to respond. 'Yes,' I agreed, my polite smile conflicting with the frown I wanted to shoot in her husband's direction. Sean was looking at the floor, his eyes closed.

'It's going to look great in the drawing room isn't it honey?'

Sean pulled his head up to answer her question with a sound I took as agreement and then his gaze flickered over to me.

My lips curled up in amusement, my eyebrows rose in question, but my spirits had plummeted. I excused myself for one moment, picked up the window cleaner, and as I walked to the office I heard Sean tell his unsuspecting wife that she'd been quick. He thought they were going to meet in the café.

Charlie was texting and looked up with a smile as I walked in. I wondered whether she and Greg were talking about baby name ideas.

'Do you need any help?' she asked.

'No, it's fine,' I assured her. 'I'm just fetching the step ladder.'

'You're not going to clean the windows are you,' she frowned, noticing the bottle in my hand.

'No, of course not, I'm going to take the tapestry down.'

At half past five I stuck a sold sticker on a kitchen cabinet and turned the sign hanging in the shop door from open to closed.

'It's getting even wilder out there,' Charlie commented as she pulled on her coat.

'Yes,' I agreed, staring out at the torrents of water running down the street. 'Wind's picking up.'

Charlie's phone rang and she dug it out of her handbag. 'Hey, yeah I'll be right there. Okay. See you in a minute. Love you, bye.'

I offered her a smile. 'Have a nice evening.'

'You too,' she replied. 'See you tomorrow.' She stepped out the door, opened up her umbrella and was gone.

Looking back into the shop and the bare wall behind the counter, I thought that in terms of business I couldn't have had a better day and yet it had made no difference to my mood. I could have sworn more women pushing prams had come into the shop that afternoon than throughout the entire last six months. I was ready to go home but wished that there was someone there waiting for me. Once I'd locked up I dashed out to my car and turned the key, but nothing happened.

'Damn it!' I cursed as I slapped the steering wheel with one hand and tried it again. 'Damn, damn, damn!'

I put my head back against the rest and took several deep breaths, telling myself to calm down. The sound of the rain hammering against the roof filled the car and I found myself thinking about Modi and hoped that he was home by now. I don't know how long I sat there watching the rain hit the windscreen and trickle down the glass, but at last I called my parents.

'Hello Harriet, climb in,' my dad smiled as I opened the car door, and he reached into the back seat and shifted a pair of anoraks out of the way.

I pulled the door to and wiped the moisture from my face on my sleeve.

'Hi,' I said. 'Thanks so much for doing this.'

'No problem,' my dad replied but I noted my mother's silence. It was only once we were out of town and up the road that she spoke.

'I don't know why you still drive that rust ridden thing,' she contributed.

I suddenly realised that I'd caught the tail end of an argument, arguments which these days were becoming a more frequent occurrence between my parents. The atmosphere was so sour I could almost taste the lemony zing on the end of my tongue. After thirty-six years of marriage I'd begun to wonder whether even their love was approaching its expiry date and the small quirks in each other's characters had, after all those years, become irritating habits that neither could stand anymore. The car jolted as my dad ran over a large pothole and I knew that, although staring out of the window, my mum had certainly noticed and was close to boiling over. I supposed after the day I'd had how could I have hoped to have anything but a strained evening as well. My mum reached for the radio as there came a lull in the classical music playing in the car and she nudged the volume up.

'How's everything going with the shop these days Hattie?' my dad asked, steering the conversation elsewhere.

'Good,' I shrugged. 'I'm happy with how things are going.'

'I miss it sometimes,' he frowned. 'Up in that workshop.'

'Nonsense Henry, you fall asleep standing up these days,' my mum interrupted. 'There's no way you'd cope with all that now.'

'Now I'm old?' he asked.

My mum didn't reply and instead reached for the radio again as the music rose to the crescendo and she nudged the volume down. By the time the piece fell to an almost inaudible level again, she turned it back up and murmured,

'This weather's dreadful.'

Returning to neutral ground was her way of waving the white flag and my dad and I agreed with the observation.

'Do you want to come in for a cup of tea?' I asked as we drew up outside my house.

'That would be lovely,' my dad smiled and we dashed from the car to the front porch.

As I opened the front door Coco ran over to greet me but then retreated when she realised I wasn't alone.

'It's all right,' I assured her as she eyed my parents cautiously. Glancing around the kitchen I spotted Mona and Flicks too and then Bea appeared in the doorway to the hall. 'Grab a seat, I'll put the kettle on,' I said but instead of walking over to the sink I went into the living room and to my dismay Modi wasn't there. I looked up the staircase, my hand clutching the banister tightly. 'Modi? Are you up there?' The patter of paws did not sound on the floorboards overhead.

I returned to the kitchen and found my dad still rubbing the soles of his shoes on the doormat.

'It's okay dad,' I told him. 'It needs a clean-up in here anyway.'

I took off my coat then flicked on the kettle and opened a packet of cookies, double chocolate. I needed something to cheer me up and apparently I wasn't the only one.

'Oh, I love these,' my dad smiled mischievously as he whisked one from the packet. 'I like that little side table I spotted in your living room the other night by the way Hattie,' he said in-between mouthfuls.

'I got it a couple of weekends back,' I replied, 'from a car boot. It had a box of old videos sitting on top of it.'

'It's amazing what you can find,' he commented.

I took a second biscuit and so did he. Meanwhile my mum waited for a cup of tea to accompany hers and once I'd poured three mugs I sat down at the kitchen table.

'Long day eh?' my dad said as I sighed with fatigue.

I nodded but I didn't feel like explaining that it was more than my car and today's weather which was weighing me down. Adding more problems to those already flying around the table wasn't going to help anything.

'How will you get to work in the morning?' my mum asked.

'There's a bus that stops in the village,' I said. 'I'll call the garage about my car when I get to the shop tomorrow.' I looked towards the window as a gust of wind hit it, carrying petals it had stripped from the flowers. 'I was hoping to do some more gardening this week,' I murmured.

'Well everything comes to an end,' my mum replied and I got the feeling she wasn't just talking about the sunshine. I glanced across at my dad, wondering whether he'd deduced the same as me.

'We're off to the theatre Wednesday night,' he said. 'Ryan and Karen got us some tickets for our anniversary.'

'Oh yeah? That should be good,' I smiled.

'Poor Karen,' my mum said, 'she's been so under the weather lately.'

'Have you seen her?' I asked.

'I spoke to her on the phone earlier,' my mum frowned, sensing my scepticism. 'Don't be so sour just because she missed your birthday party Harriet. You're not six anymore. She's got an awful cold. Says she probably caught it from that sister of hers, you know the one who works at that primary school?'

My mum continued to trace Karen's germs back as though it was a family tree and out of the corner of my eye I could see that my dad's attention had wandered to the newspaper lying open on the table near his elbow. My own gaze returned to the packet of cookies as I deliberated having a third. There was a rumble of thunder and I glanced up at the light overhead as it flickered.

'Are you going to that big antique fair this Saturday?' my dad asked, tiring of the newspaper. It was a rhetorical question really; he would have not for one moment doubted that my answer would be yes, he knew me very well. Indeed I wouldn't have doubted it either but I hesitated.

'No,' I found myself saying, 'I'm going on holiday.'

'Holiday?' my mum frowned.

'Just for a few days.'

'Where are you going?' she asked.

'And who with?' my dad added seriously. 'Have you got a boyfriend?'

'Lou told us about your date,' my mum chipped in.

'Lou what?' Suddenly my parents were a coalition force again and my little sister their snitch. 'You know what, that doesn't matter. No, I haven't got a boyfriend. I'm going to the Lake District. And on my own.'

There was a long pause as they soaked up this information.

'What for?' my mum eventually said.

'Because I want to,' I replied. 'And because I think I need to.'

She frowned. 'What does that mean?'

I sighed and realised I wasn't going to get away without an explanation. 'Do you ever feel like you're watching a race, standing on the side line cheering everyone on, but you're not taking part?'

They didn't say anything.

'Since Richard left,' I continued, 'in fact before that, somewhere in the midst of that marriage I lost track of who I am. What I want. I thought I was happy but then the carpet was whisked out from under my feet and I don't know what I've got left or where I'm headed. I need to clear my head and a change of scenery would help. Where better to go than there?'

'Don't be so hard on yourself Harriet,' my dad replied in that tone that sent me straight back to childhood and the days I'd curl up on his knee and he'd wipe away my tears. 'You *were* happy in that marriage, I've never seen you so happy. But Richard broke your heart.'

I looked down at the table and running my fingertip around the rim of my mug, I sternly told myself to keep it together.

'Take a short holiday,' he continued gently, 'by all means. But you're only twenty-nine. You'll work it out.'

'Me and your dad will nip round to check up on the cats while you're away,' my mum said once she was certain I wasn't crying.

'Thank you,' I murmured and then looking up I asked, 'More tea?'

'No thank you,' she replied quietly.

'I think we had better be off,' my dad added. 'It's turning into a storm out there.'

As they put on their coats I went to the front door and pulled it open.

'Modi?' I called, looking out into the garden being hammered by the wind and the rain.

'Who's Modi?' my dad asked, joining me in the

doorway as he pulled the zip up to his chin.

'My cat,' I said a little distractedly.

My mum joined us. 'What's the matter? Have you lost one?'

'I've not seen him today.'

'He's not lost,' my dad interrupted. 'Cat's always wander. He'll turn up before morning you mark my words.'

'I know,' I sighed. 'I'm just worried. I can't help it.'

'You wait until you have children,' my mum said. 'You'll never stop worrying again.'

My mum having unknowingly touched a nerve, I closed the door perhaps a little too viciously behind my parents after they'd left, and I strode back to the table where I snatched up another biscuit and then took the laptop into the living room.

The wind was battering the front of the house like it was a ship out at sea and I pulled the curtains to before dropping onto the sofa. As the laptop loaded up I glanced at the empty armchair across from me and tried not to think about Modi.

'Holidays to the Lake District,' I murmured as I simultaneously typed it into Google and then pressed enter with a determined stamp.

There were over eleven million hits: walking holidays; luxury hotels; Michelin star restaurants; horse trek vacations; spa weekends; campsites; self-catering cottages; the choices went on and on. I wasn't sure what I wanted and wondering where to start I clicked on one at random.

'*Painting holidays in the heart of Cumbria*,' I read aloud. 'No thanks.'

There was another rumble of thunder followed by a flash of lightning I glimpsed through a gap in the curtains. I looked back at the screen and chose another website. It gave me a list of bed and breakfasts and I clicked on a picture of a white cottage boasting amazing views and a friendly welcome. It showed me more photos and it did indeed look perfect but then reaching the bottom of the page I was stopped in my tracks; fully booked. I clicked my tongue, went back a page and tried another but again it was booked up for the next two months. Bea found me and nestled into my lap and by the time she woke up from her forty winks I was still no further. It appeared that there was nothing available at such short notice and I wouldn't be going anywhere after all.

Ready to give in and head to the kitchen to make something savoury to eat now I was saturated with sugar, I tried one more site for luck and startled Bea as I at last hissed a triumphant yes. A quaint pub bed and breakfast had one room left and for six nights from Thursday. After a quick call to Charlie I clicked 'Book' and the moment the confirmation email came through I heard the clatter of the cat flap and then the munching of cat biscuits. I pushed away the laptop and went to the kitchen.

'Modi!' I cried, crouching down beside him. He had his nose buried in the food bowl but spared a moment to look up at me. 'Where have you been?'

I stroked his back and noticing that his ginger fur was dry, I walked over to the window and looked out into the night. The rain had finally stopped and the storm was nothing but a distant rumble on a moody horizon. It was quite probable, I realised, that Modi had been sleeping in the potting shed all day, warm and dry if not a little hungry but reluctant to get his jacket wet.

'Wherever you've been, I'm glad you're back,' I told

him as I got some carrots out of the fridge, and knowing that was where the milk came from, suddenly all four girls raced over and meowed excitedly.

I obliged them; with the combination of Modi's return and the small break ahead of me, my spirits had risen and my optimism was rekindled. Having decided I'd make a mini cottage pie for just me, I grabbed some spuds from the pantry and was about to reach for a chopping board when I felt Modi brush against my leg.

'Don't you want any milk?' I asked, noticing that the girls were still lapping away nosily.

Modi meowed and wanting the attention as much as he did, I bent down and picked him up.

'It's a good job Richard's not here anyway, hey Modi? He's allergic to cats.'

FOUR

When it started raining again I sheltered under a tree and looked across Lake Windermere. The water was grey, like the sky above it but beyond that the hills were a palette of vibrant greens. I took another photo but knew I could never encapsulate the beauty within the four walls of the frame. All afternoon, like the day before it, I had chosen my route one step at a time following my curiosity rather than a map, like Alice delving deeper and deeper into an unknown wonderland, forever unsure what lay on the path ahead.

There's no need to look so worried Harriet. I promise you I can look after the shop, Charlie had told me Thursday morning when I'd dropped in before heading to the train station. The quote from the garage to fix my car was unequalled by its worth and so it seemed my only option was to bid the old gal farewell and take the train up north.

Enjoy yourself. You haven't taken a day off since... I can't remember when, Charlie had laughed.

I hadn't dare admit to her as I hovered beside the counter, glancing at the birthday card she'd given me the week before, that it wasn't the shop I was anxious about leaving but my cats. As I listened to the patter of the rain hitting the leaves overhead, I realised that for the first time it wasn't Richard I wanted to be holding but Modi. Ever since I'd taken him in I had been there for him every day, making sure he was happy and safe, and when Thursday morning came and I hugged all my cats goodbye I suddenly wasn't so sure about leaving. I filled up the food bowls again although my parents would be coming to feed them every day, and then stood stuck in the doorway, aware it was time to get going but struggling to move my feet. As the rain found its way down the back of my neck I felt guilty for having left them behind and thinking of them made my heart ache. And yet, in a strange way, I was happy. Home was no longer that cold lonely place it had become since the day Richard had left but where they were. I envisaged Modi sitting in his armchair and Flicks curled up in her basket beside the fireplace, and taking a deep breath I filled my lungs then let it all go with a smile.

Hearing voices carried towards me by the wind, I looked around until I spotted a group of four or five people in the distance. They were looking across the lake, at the boats bobbing on its surface. If there had been someone standing beside me I would have told them to look too, as the sun fought its way through a gap in the clouds and a rainbow appeared, arching its way from the green hills into the water. Suddenly I found myself thinking back to that last cup of tea I'd shared with my parents and realised that they'd love it here. As far as I knew they had never visited and as the rain stopped and I carried on across the field, I resolved to get a postcard and write to them saying that I was enjoying myself but next time we should come together. The three of us. I climbed over a stile and stopped where the grass met the tarmac of a narrow lane. To the right it began to fall away towards the lake and a couple of hundred metres to my left I could see some rooftops and chimney stacks. The postcard still on my mind, I wondered whether I'd find a shop there and so I turned left, unaware that the decision I'd made would mould more of my future than that one afternoon.

The town was larger than I'd expected and the tea shops were bustling with tourists in bright anoraks. I spotted a second hand book shop and unable to resist, I pushed the door open. As the bell rang above my head the floorboards creaked beneath my feet and I looked down the narrow but deep shop. It was crammed to the rafters, books even sitting on each tread of the staircase as I waded through to the first floor. I slid a book off the shelf, scattering dust everywhere that twinkled in a pool of late afternoon sunshine streaming through the upstairs window, and the paper was rough beneath my fingertips as I flicked through the pages. It was an old guide to the area and its contents were as quaint as the streets outside, making me smile as it encapsulated a by-gone age. I tucked it under my arm and continued foraging until my hands were full and I remembered I still had to walk back to the B&B. I put down three of the novels but kept the rest including a copy of Peter Rabbit as a souvenir and then headed for the till.

'Thank you,' I smiled as the man conscientiously placed the books in a bag and I was about to leave when I spotted the bookmarks at the end of the counter, and I found myself reaching out for one with a cat on it.

'They're one fifty,' the man said.

I was about to dig out the change when in my head all of a sudden I heard my sister laugh. 'I told you,' she cackled. 'You *are* a crazy cat lady.' I froze and wondered if it was true. Was I morphing into that old lady with a shrine-like mantelpiece devoted to the god of all things fluffy and cute? How soon would it be before I was sat alone every night doing cross-stich patterns of kittens whilst I smelt like I was wearing eau de pet shop? Gifts from assumptive family members was one thing but since when had I subconsciously begun collecting cat orientated things? Fearing for my sanity, I put back the bookmark and left the shop without looking back.

I walked on until I came to a gift shop with some postcards outside the door. Widely avoiding those with cute kittens sitting in baskets, I picked out six depicting local sights, the stand squeaking as I span it and then I went inside, picking up a stick of rock on my way to the counter.

'Do you know where I can buy some stamps?' I asked as everything was put in a bag.

'We happen to sell them here,' the woman smiled. 'Would you like a book of six?'

'Please,' I said.

When I went back outdoors I spotted a bench across the road and luckily it was dry enough to sit down. As my feet heaved a sigh of relief, I dug out a biro and chewing on the lid I pondered how to start. Writing six postcards was almost an essay length assignment and trying to make it to the end of the last one without resorting to copying the first, was always a task.

I considered myself fortunate to have the family I did. For the most part we got on well considering the mix of characters but when we didn't our parents were there to iron out the tension, always the backbone of our miniature society. But over the last few years I had begun to see this backbone bend and nowadays the arguments were more than often between themselves. When I tried to pinpoint the beginning of this change it seemed to come down to the time when Ollie, the youngest, had left home. My parents had had to share each other with six children for so long I wondered whether they'd forgotten what it was like to be just a couple again.

At last I put pen to paper, encapsulating in a few short sentences my trip so far, finishing with an invitation that they join me next time. I signed it *Love Hattie* and stuck on a stamp. By the time I heard the church bells chime five o'clock I'd finished the rest and my tongue was sick of the taste of stamps. The woman in the gift shop had told me that there was a post box a little further down the road and so I set off again and when I found it I also found a handsome tabby cat sitting on top of it. I smiled and slowly reached out a hand.

'Hey little fella,' I said.

At first he eyed me cautiously, wondering if I was a friend or foe, but once I began to tickle him under the chin he melted like butter.

'Aren't you sweet?' I whispered but then all of a sudden he stopped purring and ran away. I watched him leave with a frown, wondering what I'd done to scare him, but then looked to my right as a man stopped next to me.

'I don't think he likes me,' the man said with a smile.

'Yes, I think you're right,' I agreed, smiling too although the breath had caught in my throat.

He was a little taller than me, cleanly shaven with dark hair and darker eyes. He was of average build, not slight but not stocky, and not only was he good looking but he was still staring at me and once this had registered I dreaded to think how I looked in return, from the damp hair to the muddy boots, but there was not a lot I could do except tuck as much of the frizziness as I could behind my ear. He was also the postman and realising he'd come to empty the box, I remembered why I was there too.

'Sorry can I just post these?' I said, clumsily trying to get out of his way.

'Sure, I'll take them,' he offered.

'Thanks,' I smiled as I handed over the postcards. His hands showed endeavour and there was a plaster on his thumb.

'You don't happen to know the quickest way back to Windermere from here do you?' I asked as I looked back up. 'I'm on holiday,' I added, feeling I needed to explain.

He briefly glanced past my shoulder and then back. 'On your own?'

'Yes,' I replied and wondered whether he thought that was strange.

'Shame about the weather,' he said, showing another friendly smile.

'Well I can swim so I think I'll be all right.'

He laughed and I liked the sound and then for what must have only been a moment but felt much longer, his eyes flickered back and forth across my face until with a jolt of self-consciousness I looked away.

He cleared his throat and pulled out a bunch of keys. 'Well to get to Windermere,' he said, 'you want to head that way.'

I tried to concentrate as he rattled off the directions and nodded with more certainty than I felt when he asked,

'You got that?'

'Yes I think so,' I smiled. 'Thanks for your help.'

'No problem.'

Unless one of us said anything else I guessed this was the part when we went our separate ways and as the silence continued to stretch out I was the first to move.

'Well bye,' I said, going to turn away.

'I...' he started.

I stopped and looked back at him but that first word wasn't followed by another. His lips opened and closed again without saying anything in between and as if my heart wasn't beating fast enough, it notched up a gear as I wondered what it was he wanted to say and then what it meant if he didn't try again.

He swallowed and then a small smile which lacked the genuineness of those that had come before it, appeared on his face. 'I hope you enjoy your visit,' he said.

I didn't think we would ever cross paths again, after all what were the chances unless I timed it for five at the same post box again tomorrow? And from the look on his face when the following evening we did, it seemed he hadn't expected to see me again either.

I had been sitting near the window in the pub, watching the colours of the sunset run across the sky, when he walked through the door dressed in jeans and a blue checked shirt rolled up to the elbows. He pulled off the casual but incredibly hot look so well I wasn't even sure he'd tried. I took a sip of wine as he followed his two friends to the bar, hiding my gaze behind the glass as I felt something beneath my skin prickle.

The room was busy that evening and when he looked in my direction for a spare table I couldn't stop my gaze fleeing back out of the window. I could almost hear Lou's voice inside my head, scolding me. *Why are you hiding? You like him don't you?* But I was out of practice. My stomach was churning like someone had stuck it in a blender and when I dared to glance back across the room and found him looking straight at me, my heart started beating against my rib cage so ferociously I could have sworn it was trying to get the hell out of there. Having tamed my hair and lost the coat I wasn't even sure that he'd recognise me, but when my lips curled up into a smile, so did his.

'Hello again.'

'Hi,' I said. He'd left his friends at the pool table, choosing their cues like gladiators selecting their weapons, and asked me if I wanted some company.

'Love some,' I smiled.

'Quite a coincidence bumping into you again,' he said as he sat down. 'I'm Dan by the way.'

'Harriet,' I replied and his smile grew a little more.

'How's the holiday going Harriet?'

'I'm enjoying myself so far,' I said.

'Despite the glorious climate?'

'Well I didn't come for the weather.'

He took a sip of his drink. 'So what did bring you here?' he asked.

'It was kind of a last minute thing actually,' I explained. 'And totally not like me,' I added, shaking my head. 'I'm not usually so rash but...I needed to get away.'

I expected him to ask what from but he didn't.

Instead he said, 'You're from the Midlands aren't you?'

'It's the accent right?' I asked.

'I like it,' he replied and I laughed, wondering if he was serious. His own accent was typical of the area, confident and strong.

'I'm from the Peak District to be precise. Do you know it?'

He shook his head. 'Not really. What do you do back there?'

'I have an antique shop,' I said.

I think the look on his face was impressed mixed with surprise. 'Furniture?'

'All sorts of things,' I told him. 'Furniture, art, books, anything really. There's something intriguing about items that have been around for hundreds of years. It's kind of a passion of mine as well as work.'

'You're lucky then,' he said. 'The two rarely coincide.'

'You mean you didn't always dream of being a postman?' I jested and he laughed.

'Funnily enough, no.'

'So what is yours?' I asked. 'Passion I mean.'

He took a deep breath and said, 'I'm a photographer when I'm not delivering the mail.'

I wondered whether he could be more perfect. 'What do you photograph?'

'Animals mostly.'

I smiled and answered the question in my head with a yes. 'Like wildlife?'

'Sometimes, yeah, but also farm animals and pets. I like landscapes as well. '

'I bet that can be testing can't it? Pets are notoriously difficult to work with.'

'Yeah,' he admitted, 'but I like a challenge and the

56

results are worth it.'

'I don't doubt it,' I smiled.

'Do you have any pets?' he asked.

It should have been an easy question to answer but I hesitated, torn over telling the truth or avoiding it. If I said I had five cats he'd undoubtedly come to only one conclusion and make a run for it. Even my family who'd known me since the off had decided I'd gone a little nutty. It wasn't that I was ashamed or embarrassed but I barely knew Dan and I didn't want him to get the wrong idea.

'I have a cat called Modi,' I blurted, my decision abruptly made although technically I was just withholding information rather than lying.

'I should have guessed that huh?'

He meant the cat I'd been fussing when we'd first met at the post box.

'What about you?' I asked him.

'A hamster,' he said in a matter of fact manner.

It was so unexpected I laughed. 'Seriously?'

'Yeah,' he replied, laughing too and then as the laughter died he added, 'Well, technically he's my son's hamster.'

'Oh,' I said, my eyes widening. So there was the catch. I took another sip of wine and digested the information.

Dan fidgeted in his chair and then said, 'His name's Joe.'

'Your son I'm assuming, not the hamster.'

'Yeah, that's right,' he replied with a small smile. 'The hamster's called Indiana.'

'Jones?' I wondered.

Dan nodded and as a silence settled between us I could tell from the look on his face that he was scared I was going to bail. The prospect of getting involved with a man who already had a kid was one I had not considered before and as the negotiations for and against the idea rallied back and forth in my head, I realised that if I didn't break the silence soon I might as well have said, *Nah thanks, that sounds too much like hard work*, without even giving it a shot.

'How old is your son?' I asked.

'He's just turned five,' Dan said. 'I'm divorced.'

'Then that's something we have in common,' I told him.

It was his turn to look surprised but before he could ask any questions I changed the subject.

'Do you sell your photographs?'

'Sometimes,' he said, shrugging his shoulders, and a whisper of self-consciousness crossed his face. 'But like I said I'm not a professional. More like an enthusiastic amateur.'

I got the impression he was under-selling himself unlike Richard who had always oozed with self-confidence, a characteristic in men which I had once liked but was now tired of. 'Have you been doing it long?' I asked.

'Since I got my first camera,' he said, 'which was when I was about fourteen. It was just this cheap disposable thing but... well I was hooked. From then on I used to spend all my pocket money on developing films.'

I smiled. 'It's so beautiful here. I don't think I've ever taken as many photos in my life as during these last three days, though they're probably nowhere near as good as yours.'

He chuckled. 'You haven't seen them yet.'

I tucked my hair behind my ear. 'Does that mean

you'll show me?'

He hesitated, his eyes looking into mine, then said, 'What are you doing tomorrow afternoon?'

FIVE

A date was the last thing I had expected to find in the Lake District. After the collapse of a four year long marriage the thought of starting out on first dates again had been a daunting one, and I remembered fobbing off Lou on more than one occasion with excuses that I wasn't ready. The only time she did manage to shoehorn me out of my comfort zone was to meet a colleague of hers and the evening had done nothing to help my confidence. And yet, that Saturday afternoon, as I walked down the streets of an unfamiliar town trying to find the café where Dan had suggested we meet, I couldn't deny within the safety of my own mind that I was excited. That's if I made it on time I thought as I glanced at my watch and grimaced.

When I at last found the café, the chairs outside were already taken and the sounds of a busy kitchen resonated out of the open door. Walking inside I feared for a moment that Dan may have given up on me and already left, but then I saw him across the room.

'I'm so sorry,' I apologised as I reached his table. He stood up with a smile on his face and it only grew wider as I tried to explain how I'd struggled to find the café.

'That's okay,' he replied, looking entertained by my ramblings. He wore a grey t-shirt, jeans and boots, and he smelt as good as he looked. We sat down and I knew my cheeks were burning.

'Do you want some ice cream?' he asked.

'Ice cream?'

'You look too warm for coffee,' he offered.

It was a hot day and I was happy to let him think that's why I was glowing.

'Sure,' I smiled.

'What flavour?'

'Chocolate please,' I said and he went over to the counter then returned with two small tubs.

'This is the best ice cream ever by the way,' Dan warned me as he sat down and passed one over. 'There's a little spoon inside.'

'Thanks,' I smiled.

On the lid was a picture of a cow and peeling it off I found the promised spoon concealed inside. Dan had chosen strawberry and as we simultaneously ate the first spoon, he looked at me and smiled.

'I was right huh?' he said.

I nodded. 'Uh huh, it's good.' And it really was.

'So have you done much exploring so far?'

'Oh yeah,' I said. 'Last few days I've seen some great places.'

'Like where?' he asked curiously.

'I've just been wandering.'

He looked a little amused by my ambiguous response.

'To tell you the truth I'm not that good with maps,' I

grimaced, realising how ignorant I must sound. 'It's okay, you can laugh,' I told him.

'I wasn't going to laugh,' Dan protested despite the grin on his face. 'I was just going to say it sounds like you could use a guide.'

We both knew he meant he'd be happy to show me round but I needed to hear him say it.

'Any idea where I can find one?' I asked, smiling.

'No one knows this place like I do,' he said.

'Sounds good,' I beamed and then looking back down at my ice cream I rooted out a chocolate chip. 'So where should we go first?' I asked. 'You said you would show me your photographs.'

'I did,' he admitted.

'Do you have a studio?'

'No,' he said, shaking his head, and noticing something funny about his expression I sensed I should turn around.

Framed on the wall behind me were a series of photographs comprising of several landscapes and portraits of animals.

'Are these all yours?' I asked, looking back at him.

'Yeah,' he replied and I spotted that self-conscious look cross his face again.

'They're great,' I smiled, turning in my chair again. Directly behind me was a landscape shot. The sun was rising across a lake, the red sky reflected pink in the water and across the snow covered ground. The next photograph along was that of a cockerel, his pose suggesting he knew his portrait was being taken. His outlandish tail feathers boasted an array of colour and his deep red crest fell to one side. After that was a woodland scene in which a small path wound its way through the old thick trunks of a forest, the golden leaves of autumn tumbling from the branches to carpet the earth. The fourth in line was a portrait of a chubby lamb, his face speckled black and white. The creature's head was ever so slightly cocked to one side, and his ears were upright and alert. I wondered how many shots Dan had taken before he'd reached this perfect one and decided he must be a patient man.

'They're fantastic,' I smiled, taking my eyes off them to look back at Dan. 'And that lamb is so sweet.'

'His name's Curly,' Dan replied.

'How original,' I grinned but my smile fell as Dan added,

'He's an orphan, well kind of. His mother had two lambs and rejected one of them. The kids on the farm hand reared him.'

My heart melted.

'He's got a great personality,' Dan said. 'He'll have grown a bit since I took that.' He hesitated then asked, 'What is it?'

My mind had momentarily wandered elsewhere and he had noticed. 'Oh it doesn't matter,' I said, shaking my head.

'Sure it does.'

'No, you don't want to hear it,' I told him.

Again he looked tickled by my squirming. 'I do. Tell me.'

I opened my mouth and eventually said, 'Curly just reminded me of someone.'

'Who?'

I made a little laugh, feeling awkward. I had failed to meet one man yet who was fond of cats and I knew it was a bad idea to mention them. But he wasn't going to let it go so what could I do? 'He reminded me of Modi,' I said quietly.

'Your cat, right?'

I nodded and decided I better explain. 'He's an orphan too, well kind of,' I added, mimicking Dan's choice of words. 'I found him in a cardboard box in the corner of a car park. He'd been dumped next to the bins, like he was rubbish.' My gaze drifted to the right, gazing into nothingness. 'He was so small, so helpless.'

'And you took him in.'

I nodded again. My dad teased me about my cats, my mum looked on with a frown. Others like Sian found it amusing and then my sister Lou insisted it was a bad idea. If I'd been afraid that Dan might react in the same way or simply be far from interested, I needn't have. He was still looking at me, attentive of every word.

'Then he's lucky you found him,' Dan said. 'He's not an orphan anymore.'

I smiled and looked down at my tub of ice cream. It was melting around the edge, against the warmth of my fingertips, and I ate another spoon.

'Have you ever been on a boat?' Dan asked. 'Here on the lakes I mean.'

I shook my head.

'It's the best way to see them,' he said.

I liked the idea. 'Can we hire one nearby?'

'I can do one better.'

The sky was cloudless overhead and the sun warm on our backs as we stepped side by side onto a wooden pier, our arms just not brushing one another.

'You have a boat?' I asked as my gaze picked out a nearby yacht.

He shot me a grin. 'I'm afraid it's not that one. It's a little more rustic than that.'

'Well I happen to love rustic,' I smiled.

He stopped next to a small motor boat, a little tired in appearance but clearly in the midst of refurbishment.

'Here she is,' he said, looking back at me to catch my first impressions.

'It's great,' I smiled. 'Are you doing all the work yourself?'

'Yeah,' he said, his hands on his waist. 'Bit by bit.' His gaze ran over the chipped paint with a glow of pride and then he stepped aboard, turning back to me with his hand outstretched.

'Come on, I'll teach you how to drive,' he smiled.

I reached out, feeling the hard callused skin of his hand against mine for the first time, and stepped across the gap.

'Okay?' he asked as the boat swayed and the water slapped against the side.

I nodded. 'Let's go.'

Feeling Dan's eyes on me, I looked up from the wheel and glanced across at him.

'You're a natural,' he smiled.

I couldn't imagine steering a small boat across a large lake was a tricky task for anyone, there wasn't exactly anything to bump in to, but I was still appreciative of the compliment. My boating experience was limited to kayaking as a child and once out in the open I remembered that sense of freedom being out on the water brought. Beyond the hum of the engine all I could hear was the gentle churning of water and looking out, I watched the furrows of small waves radiate out across the surface from the prow of the boat. I was glad we'd escaped the crowds and shielding my eyes from the sun I gazed around the lake from a whole new angle. It was so peaceful but still my heart was racing, my stomach uneasy but not from the water. It had been a long time since such adrenaline had coursed my veins, so long since I'd felt the rush of meeting someone new and not knowing what lay ahead, that I think I'd almost forgotten what it felt like.

'Head over that way,' Dan said, reaching for the wheel to steer me in the right direction. His hand touched mine for a second time and I pretended not to notice.

'Do you come out here often?' I asked him.

'As much as I can,' he replied, squinting as he looked back at me. 'Though it's not usually as enjoyable as today.'

At first I thought he meant because of the weather then realised he was talking about me and my lips curled up into a shy smile. We were quite a way out into the lake by then. I could see the occasional tour boat in the distance but the boats closer by were those of fisherman and locals.

'Have you always lived here?' I asked him.

'Almost, yes,' he nodded, 'except for when I spent eighteen months in Manchester for work.'

'What kind of work?'

'I'm a mechanic...or used to be. A friend of mine there offered me a job at his garage after I got divorced. He'd known me since we were kids together. I thought I'd make a fresh start somewhere new.'

'But it didn't work out?'

'I missed Joe,' Dan said simply. 'I barely got to see him. I enjoyed the work but I didn't get on with the city either. I like space and quiet. I decided I'd rather be a postman back where I belonged than what I was doing.'

'So that's what you did,' I smiled.

'That's what I did,' he repeated, his smile as well as

his words mirroring mine. 'I don't have much family so I have to hold onto all I've got.'

I was trying to imagine what Joe was like. If he was anything like his dad then I decided he must be the sweetest kid in the whole world.

Dan told me he didn't have any siblings and his father had passed away four years ago, then suddenly it was my turn and I filled him in on the basics, needless to say avoiding all mention of my marriage, and I was glad that when it came to *any questions,* he didn't ask about it.

'You're one of six?' he said, looking surprised.

'Yes. Number three if you were wondering.'

'I can't imagine a house that full,' he smiled. 'Do you all get on?'

'Within reason,' I shrugged. 'I probably get on with my dad best of all.'

He looked even more surprised at that.

'He was the one who started the shop,' I told him.

'Your antique shop?' Dan asked.

'Yes. When I was younger I used to help out at weekends. We'd go to the markets and antique fairs together, just the two of us. He taught me what to look out for and how to repair it if it was damaged and before I knew it I'd caught the bug. After college I began working there full time.'

We both looked right as a fish jumped out of the water and as we watched the ripples left behind on the surface of the lake slowly fade, Dan said, 'My dad loved fishing. Unfortunately we didn't get on so well.' His brow creased into a frown but he shrugged it off and then nodded up ahead. 'Do you see that up there?'

A tower stood on the brink of the hill, silhouetted against the blue sky.

'Yes,' I replied.

'It's an old ruin.'

'Haunted?'

'If you believe in such things,' Dan grinned, 'which I'm afraid I don't.'

'I'm not sure if I do,' I said. 'I just like the stories.'

We decided to moor the boat up at an old dilapidated pier and venture on foot to the ruin. I stepped out of the sun and into the shade of the trees growing along the bank with a sigh of relief. I hadn't expected it to get so hot but despite the heat wave the ground was still incredibly soft underfoot.

'Maybe this wasn't such a good idea,' Dan said as the mud began to get deeper and trickier to negotiate. 'Do you want to turn back?'

'No,' I said, shaking my head. 'It'll be all right.' I was a country girl and no amount of mud had ever stopped me before.

'Okay, I'll go first,' Dan said.

He chose his path carefully and I followed, pulling a face as my feet sank deeper and deeper with each step. It would be an uncomfortable journey back if I fell over, not to mention embarrassing.

'Are you all right?' Dan called over his shoulder as I reached what seemed to be the nucleus.

'I think so,' I replied but then as I tried to pull my right foot out of the mud, fighting against the suction as the ground made a loud squelching sound, I realised I wasn't. 'Oh no!' I shrieked. 'I think I'm stuck.'

'Hang on, I'm coming back,' Dan replied.

I tried to wriggle my foot free but the mud just seemed to swallow it more, tightening around my boot. I began to wobble and swore I was going to fall.

'No you're not,' Dan said as he reached me and

grabbed my arm.

'Thanks,' I smiled, reassured by his strength as he held me steady. I looked up into his face, realising we were closer than we'd ever been, and he stared back, the eye contact only broken when I glanced back down at our feet. 'Now what?' I said.

He cleared his throat, then said, 'You go first.'

I began trying to loosen my right foot and eventually heaved it free, the mud letting it go with a loud squelch.

'Keep going,' Dan said.

The mud released my left foot without too much difficulty once the other was free and once I'd escaped the bog I suddenly had three inch platforms of mud. I looked from my feet back to Dan. He was still standing there, as stuck as I had been. He wobbled back and forth and I admired his balance as he managed to stay upright. Slowly he negotiated his first foot free but then when he tried to pull out the second he came away with only his sock.

'Damn it,' he said, hobbling on one leg.

I tried to hide my smile by pinching my lips together but when this time he lost his balance and first his foot, then knee, and a hand went down into the mud, he looked up at me with a smile broader than mine.

'This is all your fault,' he grinned. 'Look at me now!'

'My fault?' I said laughing. 'You're the guide. I was following you.'

He started laughing too and with tears in my eyes I watched him pull himself back up out of the mud. 'I don't suppose you've got a spare boot on you, have you?' he joked as we looked back at his buried almost to the cuff.

'Didn't your mum always tell you to tie your laces?' I called, wondering if they hadn't been loose whether he'd have lost it.

'I rushed back to rescue you,' he said in his defence.

'And I'm eternally grateful,' I smiled.

His gaze lingered on mine for longer than I'd expected and I felt myself blush and then abruptly he turned away as though pondering what to do about his boot.

'Here,' I said, picking up a long stick. I held it out towards him and then tightly onto a tree branch with my other hand. He grabbed the end of the stick and using it to steady himself, leant back out for his boot without having to step back into the deep mud.

'Got it,' he said as I heard the mud squelch. He pulled a face as he pushed his foot back into the boot and I tried to stop myself giggling as he hobbled out of the mud.

'I know you're laughing,' he smiled.

'So are you!' I sniggered but then the smile vanished from my face as he reached for my hand. My stomach jolted and my heart began to pound in that excited but simultaneously terrified way. Dan had stopped laughing too but when I looked at him he smiled and squeezed my hand.

'You okay?'

I nodded and the smile slowly returned to my face. 'I was just thinking we've got to come back this way.'

'Well we can hardly get any muddier can we?' he smirked, looking down at our feet. 'Come on,' he said and we continued along the footpath.

Dan told me that the best time to visit the ruin was at dawn, when the sky was red and sometimes a mist crept around the footings of the old stone. I said I'd have to take his word for it because I never got up that early. So we shared the ruin with a host of other

70

sightseers that afternoon, their children darting through doorways and playing hide and seek amongst what was left of the old rooms.

When we perched on a stone wall to rest our feet, I hid a smile as Dan tried to brush some of the mud off his jeans with the back of his hand.

'You've got some on your face,' I said, pointing to my own right cheek.

He tried to wipe it off but missed.

'Up a bit,' I said.

'Gone?'

I shook my head and reaching out, wiped it off with my thumb. As my hand fell back to my side he just stared at me and with a sudden jolt of self-consciousness I looked away. Swallows were racing across the sky, singing in the warmth of the sun. I watched them weave in and out of the old walls, my stomach doing just as many somersaults.

'When do you leave?' I heard Dan ask and I looked back at him.

'In three days,' I said and already I knew that would come too soon.

SIX

I rarely remembered my dreams but when I did they were nightmares. I'd woken with a start at six am and looked around my room in the bed and breakfast unsure for several long moments where I was, and it was only when I saw my suitcase sitting beside a chair and remembered that I was on holiday, that the fears which had wrestled me from my sleep resurfaced. It had been a nightmare which set my heart pounding and thoughts spinning even when I was awake and knowing sleep wouldn't have me back, I pushed away the covers and climbed out of bed. Me and the world never usually got to see that much of each other at that time of the morning but cracking open the window and feeling the fresh air of the day on my face, I was glad not to have missed seeing the street outside slowly wake up. From my window I could count four cats of different colours and sizes, always the residents of every neighbourhood first up or last to bed, depending on how you looked at it. One little fella sitting in a plant pot and using the flower inside it as a cushion, looked quite a bit like Modi and my mind began spinning in dangerous circles again as I thought about my dream until I sternly told myself to stop it. *He was fine. It was just my imagination.*

I was the first down to breakfast and one cup of tea and a croissant later I headed outdoors. I was meeting Dan again later, same place as the day before, but I'd noticed on my way there yesterday an intriguing little junk shop. I had plenty of time to check it out and on the way I would make the call that was on my mind.

'Hello,' said my dad in his cheery telephone voice.

'Hi it's Hattie,' I told him.

'Oh hiya. How's it going?'

'Good thanks,' I replied, smiling as I heard my mum in the background ask who it was on the phone.

'It's Harriet,' my dad called back to her and I recoiled as his voice boomed a little louder into the receiver than I expect he'd known. 'And what have you been up to?' he asked me, volume back to normal.

'Just walking and sightseeing.' The question I wanted to ask was on the tip of my tongue but I didn't want to skip the usual stuff for fear of seeming rude. Fortunately my dad brought it up for me.

'Your cats are fine by the way.'

'They are?' I said, the weight instantly falling from my shoulders.

'Yeah, no problems. I think they miss you but other than that all's well.'

I felt a pang of heartache.

'Tell you what that little grey one's greedy,' my dad added.

I laughed, thinking of Mona.

'And that ginger one-'

'Modi!' I heard my mum interrupt.

73

'Yeah that one,' my dad carried on, 'he just sleeps all the time.'

My hand tightened around the phone and I wished I was holding him.

'So everything's definitely okay?' I heard myself ask again.

'Well I didn't see the spotty one,' my dad said thoughtfully.

'Coco?' I asked, instantly worried.

'Yes we did,' my mum but in again. 'They were all there. All five of them. I counted.'

'I stand corrected,' my dad said to me. 'Your mum says they were all there.'

'Good,' I replied, mainly to myself.

'And you,' my dad then said. 'You're being careful out there aren't you?'

'Of course dad,' I replied, smiling to myself.

'Don't go getting lost and I hope you've got plenty of water with you because it's been very hot.'

'Yes I have and besides I have a guide so I won't get lost.'

There was a pause. 'A guide? Who?'

'Just this local guy,' I shrugged.

Instantly I could tell that my dad was suspicious but I wasn't going to say any more about Dan.

'Honestly I'm fine,' I assured him. 'I'm having fun.'

'You sound happy,' he admitted.

'Well like I said, I just needed a break.'

I came to a standstill outside the junk shop and looked through the window. It was dingy and crowded inside; perfect conditions for hunting.

'Harriet?'

'What was that dad?' I asked.

'I said make sure you visit Furness Abbey. It's

74

supposed to be fantastic.'

'Yeah I will do,' I replied.

'Well I'll let you get off,' my dad said, 'you sound busy.'

'Okay, thanks for checking up at home for me.'

'No problem. Speak soon.'

'Yeah, speak soon dad. Love you.'

'Love you Hattie.'

I slid my phone back into the pocket of my jeans and then, with my breath held in anticipation, I stepped into the junk shop. It was cool inside and my footsteps made no sound on the tiled floor. I heard a woman say hello but looking around struggled to see anyone amongst the waves of oddities until a small lamp drew my eye to the base of a staircase where I finally spotted an old dear tucked behind a desk with a paperback novel.

'Hello,' I replied.

She'd reached the point where she was struggling for room long ago and choosing my steps carefully, slowly I tiptoed along the narrow path that had been left to snake through her large and varied collection of things, some of which was indeed junk. But for me the greatest appeal of my job was the chase and my gaze dancing from left to right, I had long ago honed the skill of spying out anything special.

That day, amongst the dusty old boxes of books, rails of vintage clothes, and the largest collection of crockery I'd ever set eyes on, I got the feeling that there was something waiting to be found and it wasn't long before I discovered that I was right. When my gaze fell on an old chest of drawers my feet simultaneously came to a halt. Although half buried and in need of a good polish, I could see it was a quality piece of furniture. I reached out and touch the wood, dull beneath a good many layers of dust, then looked back at the old dear reading at her desk and wondered if she knew what she had. Perhaps she did and it was still in the shop because she had priced it so high. On the other hand if it was affordable there was no way I could get it back home. Negotiations wheeling in my head, in the end I walked away without asking, telling my feet to keep going even though it wasn't what I wanted. It was easier to walk away not knowing than having tried on the perfect dress and not been able to buy it.

Dan was sitting outside the café, just like he said he'd be, and from what I could tell he was subtly photographing a small Yorkshire terrier which was sitting on an old lady's knee and peering at him cheekily over her shoulder from a nearby table. It was the little dog who spotted me first and then Dan's gaze followed his.

'Hey,' he said, smiling as he stood up.

'Hi. I see you've made a new friend,' I grinned.

'Yeah,' he laughed, and then pulled over a chair for me. 'Do you want a drink?'

'I'll have a coffee,' I said as I sat down.

The day had started out hazy but slowly the sun was beginning to break through and I expected it to be another scorcher. Dan returned with two steaming coffees and I stirred in a sugar cube.

'Can I have that?' he asked, meaning the second sugar cube I didn't want.

'Sure,' I said, handing it over, but rather than stirring it into his coffee he pocketed it.

'It might come in handy later,' he explained when spotting my bemused expression.

'What for?' I asked.

'It's for a friend of mine,' Dan replied. 'Toby.'

Toby turned out to be a Shetland pony with a chestnut brown coat and a black mane, and as soon as he spotted us he trotted over to the fence and sniffed Dan's camera with large pink nostrils. Dan reached out to pat him on the neck and stepping up to the fence I stroked his forehead where a white dart parted the brown fur.

'Toby, meet Harriet,' Dan said.

'He's adorable,' I smiled.

Toby's ears pricked up as he spotted the sugar cube and eagerly he crunched it between his teeth. 'He'll happily pose for photographs,' Dan told me, 'until I run out of treats anyway. Here, do you want a go?'

'Err...' I stumbled as he offered me his camera. 'I don't know what to do. Holiday snaps are about my limit.'

'There are no rules,' he said. 'Just have a go.'

I took the camera and it was a lot heavier than I'd expected. 'Wow this is like weight training. And there are so many buttons,' I laughed.

'You only need to worry about that one,' he said, pointing out the shutter, 'and use the viewfinder rather than the screen,' he suggested.

I looked into it but Toby was just a large brown blur. 'How do I focus?' I frowned.

'Oh sorry,' he said, taking it back as he murmured something about changing the settings from manual to automatic. He handed the camera back. 'There you go.'

This time a Shetland appeared out of the kaleidoscope mesh of colours and Dan offered Toby another sugar cube to keep his attention as I took a picture.

'Not bad,' Dan smiled as we both looked at it on the screen.

'I bet you're never in photos yourself,' I said.

'No,' he admitted.

I took a step back so I could get them both in and pressed the shutter again. 'Then it's about time you were,' I grinned.

He looked a bit embarrassed, as though he was perfectly content with remaining behind the camera, but he was very photogenic and I told him so.

'I don't believe that,' he laughed.

I took a few more shots of Toby, playing around with the zoom and then viewed them back, but going one too far I found a photo of whom I assumed was Joe. I shot a glance over at Dan but he was busy patting Toby's neck and didn't notice. The little boy had dark hair, brown eyes and rosy red cheeks, and he was proudly sitting with his birthday cake aglow with five candles. Quickly I turned the camera off, feeling guilty or something like that for not admitting that I'd pried, even though it had been accidentally.

'You okay?' Dan asked.

'Yeah, course,' I said, gathering a smile.

Joe looked just like him and suddenly I found myself wondering why his mother and Dan had broken up. In that brief moment I'd seen further into Dan's life than I'd yet been invited to and suddenly I was unsure if I was comfortable with seeing any more. Perhaps because if I knew everything about him, he would have to know everything about me too.

'Here you are,' I said, giving Dan back the camera. He took it but held onto my hand and a genuine smile replaced the uneasy one I had tried to feign.

'I grew up not far from here,' he said once we'd left

Toby with an apple and carried on along the road.

'Oh yeah?'

We were exploring the heart of a dramatic valley dotted with farms and other walkers like us taking advantage of the good weather.

'My best friend lived at that farm over there,' he said, nodding up ahead. 'We were always roaming these hills. He had this little dog that used to follow us everywhere.'

We came to a small stream, the sunlight dancing across the surface and the water so clear you could see the pebbly bed, and I kicked off my pumps and dipped in my toes. It was cold and even though refreshing, I couldn't stop myself making a small squeal. I ventured out a little further, until the water was up to my ankles, and then looked back at Dan.

'You coming?'

He'd already taken off his shoes but looked reluctant to roll up his jeans and when he did I guessed why.

'Can you pretend you didn't see that?' he asked, glancing from the tattoo on his ankle back to me.

It was a number thirteen, only small but I didn't need to ask to know that he regretted it.

'A reminder of my rebellious days,' he explained, grimacing a little.

'You were a bad boy once hey?' I grinned.

He chuckled and stepped into the water, trying not to wince as it was colder than he'd expected. 'A long time ago,' he said, 'as you can probably tell,' he added with another laugh.

We began walking downstream, appreciating the dabbled shade of the young trees on the bank. Two squabbling sparrows erupted out of a bush and I watched them dart across our path, and then I noticed what lay up ahead.

'Is that a waterfall,' I said.

Dan said it was. As we got closer we stepped out of the stream and continued along the bank, the earth smooth and cool beneath our bare feet. The stream ran into a large pool surrounded by caves and the waterfall cascaded down the rock on the other side.

'Throw in a coin and your wish will come true,' Dan said. 'Or at least that's what they say,' he added, smiling.

I knew I had a penny in my pocket and I dug it out, then flicked it up with my thumb. With a small splash it hit the surface and then slowly the coin floated down to the depths of the pool where even the light couldn't reach it.

'What did you wish for?' Dan asked.

I'd wished he liked me as much as I did him but looking across at Dan I told him I couldn't say. 'If I do it won't come true,' I explained. I wasn't superstitious at all but I wasn't going to tell him the truth either and I think Dan knew.

'I wonder how many pennies are down there,' he said, gazing at the uneasy surface.

I could imagine the rocky bed carpeted in many layers of coins, the metal of most dulled with time but each still shimmering with the wish of the one who had cast it down there.

'And how many of those wishes came true,' I added.

As though he had read my thoughts, Dan turned to me with the faintest smile and pulled me closer until my hands were on his chest and I was utterly intoxicated by his scent, adrenaline shooting like electric through every tingling nerve. Not that long ago I had dared to wonder whether I would ever become *someone's* again. I had been cheated of happiness and convinced that I faced a loveless future, but as Dan's hands fell to my waist and his lips softly kissed mine, I knew that I was being given a second chance and my whole body responded to the touch as though it had been reawakened by a bolt of energy, and I wanted him, needed him, to kiss me again. My hands around his neck, his hair between my fingers, he responded with equal desire, and when I again looked into his eyes, I knew that at least one wish cast into the waterfall had come true.

SEVEN

I looked from the hills back to my paper and frowned. I hadn't drawn in years but something deep inside had persuaded me that morning to buy a sketch pad and pencil and rediscover what I used to love. But sitting on the grass, gazing across a spectacular landscape, I began to wonder whether through years of neglect I had forgotten how. Sighing I turned the page, abandoning my efforts so far, and looked at a fresh sheet of paper. It didn't help that my mind was stuck on Dan. I was falling for him fast and could think of nothing else, and the beauty of the lakes suddenly seemed diluted without him for company. I looked at my watch again, counting down the hours until he finished work and then hearing voices I looked back over my shoulder and spotted a couple walking across the field. They didn't notice me and reaching a fallen tree they sat down on it side by side. Inspired I stopped chewing my pencil and began sketching, finishing the piece in five minutes by which time they had moved on, unaware of the snapshot of their lives I had captured. The drawing wasn't extensively detailed but it encapsulated the moment and for the first time since setting pencil to paper that day, I smiled.

Looking up I could see that grey clouds were beginning to creep across the sky and climbing to my feet I swung my bag over my shoulder. Rain wasn't expected but I decided to continue on my way anyway. I'd left my bike, hired from a place in town, propped up against the field gate and having put my sketch book in the basket on the front, I began back down the lane. I was used to hills and knew the best thing about riding up them was free peddling down the other side and as I did I appreciated the breeze in my face, whisking the hair from my shoulders, but the pleasure of it was cut short when turning a bend my foot slipped off the peddle, the front tyre skidded on loose gravel, and I fell off.

I slowly picked myself up off the tarmac as an intense burning sensation surged from my left knee and elbow, and I grimaced as I dared to look at my injuries. Blood trickled down my leg from a large cut on my knee and although my elbow didn't look as terrible it still hurt like hell. Hissing through my teeth I tried to brush away the dirt but couldn't bare it and abandoned the task. Looking back down at my bike, lying contorted on the verge, I saw that my sketch book had been thrown from the basket and lay sprawled across the road, and hobbling over to it I groaned as I bent down to pick it up.

'This is just great,' I muttered to myself. 'I look a state.' Plus the chain had come off and I still had to get back to town.

'What happened?' Dan said, his smile falling when he saw me.

I was sitting on a bench trying to disguise my pain and although I'd tried to mop up some of the blood on a tissue I must have looked a mess. He'd not long finished work and was still wearing his uniform, just like when we'd first met, and he sat down next to me with a worried look on his face.

'I fell off a bike,' I reluctantly admitted. 'Which is something I haven't done since I was about five,' I added. 'I feel so stupid.'

'It can happen to anyone,' he told me. 'Are you badly hurt? That knee looks really painful,' he frowned.

It was throbbing so bad my eyes were brimming with tears but I ordered them to stay back.

'Not too bad. My knee and my elbow hurt,' I said.

'Come on, let's sort you out.'

He helped me up and I hobbled over to his car where I sank into the passenger seat.

'It's only a short drive home,' he assured me.

We pulled up outside the first house in a row of half a dozen, each built of grey stone with a small front garden. A white rose tumbled around the green front door and hearing a splash hit the ground I looked up and spotted a pair of chubby pigeons having a bath in the guttering.

'Take a seat,' Dan said as we walked into the kitchen. 'I'll be right back.'

I did and when he disappeared my gaze wandered around the room. A stove stood in the fireplace and on the pale yellow walls hung a couple of photographs. A child's drawing was stuck on the fridge and above the tidy kitchen worktop was a busy bookshelf. I heard his footsteps again in the next room and then he walked back through the door with a first aid kit and a wet flannel.

'Ready?' he said as he knelt down next to my chair.

I nodded and gently he began cleaning the broken skin but despite his attentiveness I still had to pinch my lips together.

'Sorry,' he said when he saw my face.

'It's okay,' I murmured, eager to see it behind a bandage and once it was he turned his attention to my elbow.

'Would you like a Mister Men plaster or a normal one for that?' Dan asked as he rummaged through the first aid bag.

I found myself smiling as he produced a box of brightly coloured plasters reserved usually for Joe. 'I don't mind,' I replied.

'Mr Happy it is then,' he decided and he stuck it on my elbow.

'Thank you,' I smiled, and I bent my arm a couple of times as though testing the repair.

'Are you hungry?' Dan asked as he stood back up. 'I could cook us some dinner if you like?'

I nodded. 'That sounds great.'

'Okay, I'm just going to get changed first.'

While he was gone a peculiar noise drew my eye to the corner of the room and spotting a hamster cage I climbed to my feet.

'Hello Indiana,' I said as I spotted the little creature racing round in his wheel.

He was brown with a white belly and his home an extravagant labyrinth of plastic tunnels and chambers. I smiled as he stopped running and stared at me with large dark eyes.

'Aren't you cute?' I murmured.

His nose to the plastic we gazed at one another and then he hopped out of the wheel and into a tunnel, heading for the food bowl.

'Just like Mona,' I smiled to myself.

'Indiana and I were just getting acquainted,' I told Dan as he reappeared wearing a dark t-shirt and jeans. 'He's got quite a set-up.'

Dan laughed. 'Yeah, Joe chose it. Nothing but the best for little Indiana.'

I grinned and followed him over to the kitchen counter, accepting a glass of wine when he offered me one.

'So what do you say to spaghetti?' he asked.

'Perfect. What can I do?'

'You don't have to do anything,' he said.

'But I want to,' I frowned. 'I'm useless at being idle.'

'Okay, well you can be in charge of carrots and I usually give Indiana a few chunks. Feel free to stick the radio on too if you want.'

I reached for the radio first and whilst tuning it in found a song I knew very well.

'You like these?' Dan asked as he returned from the fridge with the vegetables.

'Uh huh,' I nodded. 'Why so surprised?'

'I just didn't take you for a rock fan.'

'Well I make an exception for my brother's band.'

For a moment Dan looked nonplussed and when he did manage to speak, the words never made it into a full sentence. He cleared his throat and tried again.

'Are you saying you know these?'

Grinning, I took the chopping board off him which he was still holding mid-air. 'The drummer, Ollie,' I told him, 'he's my brother. My little brother.'

'No way,' Dan said, his frown turning into a smile. 'They're huge.'

'Yeah they've done well,' I smiled broadly. 'I'm proud of him.'

I took another sip of wine and Dan continued to shake his head in disbelief.

'Do you have any other famous siblings I should know about?' he asked light-heartedly.

I laughed and reached for the peeler. 'No. They're all pretty creative but Ollie's the only famous one.

'You know,' Dan said, his expression as he looked up from dicing onions suggesting that whatever he was about to tell me was a story he didn't repeat often, 'when I was a kid I used to want to play the drums.'

'Oh yeah,' I grinned.

'I dreamed of being in a rock group and I pestered and pestered but I never got lessons.' I watched him smile to himself at a memory and then he shared it. 'I used to gather stools and dustbin lids together from all over the house and arrange them like a drum kit. Then I played them with two wooden spoons.'

I pinched my lips together, trying to keep a straight face but then Dan started laughing.

'It must have sounded so dreadful,' he said and I couldn't help but giggle along. Gradually our laughter died but Dan's story wasn't finished. 'As I got older I grew out of it until I was about sixteen,' he said, 'and I got a job washing the pots at this restaurant. Suddenly I was earning my own money and I got it into my head that I wanted to drum again but for real this time. So I saved and saved and at last I bought a drum kit.' He shook his head, still smiling. 'I think that craze lasted about a fortnight. For the next two years it just sat in the corner of my bedroom. Silly huh?'

I shook my head. 'No. Sometimes things just don't work out the way we'd planned.'

He looked at me as though to say he knew all about that and I glanced at the drawing stuck to the fridge. I didn't know how often it was Joe stayed at his dad's but I got the impression that for Dan, it wasn't often enough, and I found myself feeling thankful that at least a child hadn't been caught up in the heartache of my own divorce. It had been hard enough getting through it as it was.

'The best thing about this place is the view,' Dan said.

Shielding my eyes from the late afternoon sun, I followed him out into the back garden. Beyond the tidy lawn and small plastic slide the land fell away in waves of fields and forest.

'It's beautiful,' I smiled as I sat across from him at the table on the terrace.

He topped up my wine and then his own. As we ate, a pale crescent moon hung overhead, still waiting for the sun to set, and by the time twilight came we were sitting side by side on a blanket, Dan's arm folded around me as a gentle breeze blew across the garden.

'I don't want to leave tomorrow,' I murmured.

'Then don't,' Dan replied, turning his face and kissing me on the forehead.

'I have to,' I said.

We heard an owl hoot and then another answer its call.

'Then will you let me visit you?' he asked.

I wanted nothing more but then I remembered my white lie and panicked.

'Is that a no?' he asked, noting my silence.

'No it's not that,' I rushed. 'It's just...'

He turned to look into my eyes. 'What?'

In the split second I had to make up my mind, I weighed up my two options and the chances of coming out of either unscathed. 'It's just I fibbed once...about my cat.'

He frowned. 'What do you mean?'

'I thought you might think I was crazy if I told you the truth,' I stumbled.

Dan was frowning but smiling at the same time and waited for me to elaborate.

'I actually have five.'

He looked surprised. 'Cats?'

'Yes, but it's not what it sounds like,' I hurriedly added.

'What does it sound like?'

I looked away and clenched my teeth.

'Hey,' Dan said, his finger under my chin, persuading me to look back at him. 'I don't make assumptions,' he said, suddenly serious.

'It's just that I tell people I've adopted five kittens and suddenly they think I'm this crazy cat lady,' I explained, swallowing hard. 'But they weren't there. They didn't find them, huddled in that old box. They'd been abandoned and I had no choice but to take them home, but it's a choice I've never regretted.'

At first Dan said nothing, he just looked at me, and my heart pounded more fiercely with every second that vanished without trace between us.

'If anyone can understand what you did, it's me,' Dan smiled.

I wasn't sure what he meant. 'You have a cat as well?'

'No,' he said, 'but I guess I'm quite like them.'

'You sleep a lot and like milk?' I asked, still unsure what he was talking about.

'No,' he smiled. 'I was a foundling.'

I wasn't sure what to say so I didn't say anything but my thoughts tugged my expression into a frown.

'Just like you found your cats, someone found me.'

I couldn't believe what he was saying and the first thing I heard myself ask was, 'Where?'

'In a bus stop,' he said.

I shook my head, trying to fend off the image. 'That's horrible. It's bad enough when people abandon animals but, babies...? Who would do such a thing?'

Dan shrugged. He seemed so casual about it he confused me.

'Doesn't it bother you?' I asked.

'Yes it did. Once,' he admitted. 'When I was a teenager I wanted to know why, where I'd come from, who'd abandoned me. All that kind of stuff. But I didn't realise that I was taking out the frustration of not knowing on the two people who actually cared. My parents adopted me when I was a few months old. Now I know that the biology of it doesn't matter. They're my family. They were the ones who raised me and loved me. The woman who left me in that bus shelter...she didn't care. If I ever found her no doubt I'd wish I hadn't. My only regret,' he said as a shadow crossed his face, 'is not telling my dad that. It was only when he passed away that I snapped out of it.'

Remembering the tattoo I found it hard to imagine a Dan like that. I had grown to know a thoughtful man who was relaxed and patient, but peering beneath the surface for the first time I was beginning to see that he hadn't always been that way. When he'd once told me that he didn't have much family, I hadn't fully known what he'd meant and it was suddenly clearer to me why Dan might find his job as a father to Joe particularly difficult. He had grown up with two; the one he'd never known and the one he'd pushed away. Now it was his turn to be the father and he wanted to make amends. Make sure he did it right.

'I know you're not crazy Harriet,' he said, brushing the hair from my face. 'Having a few more than the ordinary number of cats doesn't dictate sanity. You just care and I expect those five kittens are very well looked after.'

'They're the only reason why I have to go back,' I admitted. 'But I want you to come. As soon as you can.'

He reached for my hand and interlocked his fingers in mine. 'I will.'

EIGHT

'Hey Modi,' I cried, striding over to the armchair as he yawned and stretched his paws.

'I see he gets a bigger hello than I do,' I heard my dad say.

Kneeling on the floor beside the chair, fussing Modi with all ten fingers, I glanced back at my dad standing in the living room doorway with his hands in his pockets and an expression on his face that said he thought his daughter was mad.

'I brought you rock,' I said in my defence with a smile.

My dad grinned and sat down in the other armchair.

'I missed you so much,' I whispered looking back at Modi, my lips close to his face so only he could hear me. He nuzzled against my cheek as though saying the same.

'So you had a good time then?'

I turned back to my dad and Modi hopped off the chair and sat next to me on the carpet, rubbing his nose against my knee. 'Yeah,' I said. 'It was great.'

'Did you go to Furness Abbey?'

I grimaced, having forgotten he'd mentioned it. 'I wanted to but I ran out of time. There's so much to see. It's really beautiful.'

'Did you meet many people?'

By that he meant did I meet *anyone* and he already knew the answer, my smile gave it away, but he was feigning ignorance.

'The couple who owned the bed and breakfast were lovely,' I said. 'Everyone was friendly really. I think you'd like it there. Did you get my postcard?'

'Yes,' he replied but when he didn't elaborate I wondered whether my suggestion of a trip there together sometime had gone down like a ton of bricks.

'So where did you say mum was?' I asked.

'Oh she's gone to visit Ryan and Karen. She'll be back Friday.'

I nodded, wondering if there was more to my mum's spontaneous trip than met the eye but didn't comment, then Modi clambered onto my knee and my smile reappeared. He could always do that.

'Well your break seems to have done the trick,' my dad said. 'It's good to see you smiling again Hattie. Anyone would think you were in love.'

Our gazes met and despite trying so hard to keep my expression even, this time I broke under the pressure.

'Don't worry, I won't tell a soul,' he winked.

'Tell what?' I grinned. 'There's nothing to tell. I haven't said a word. I'm just happy to see my cats...and you of course,' I quickly added.

He laughed, entirely unconvinced on both counts.

'You want to stay for dinner?' I asked.

'Why not?'

*

I lifted the lid off the steamer and poked a carrot but it wasn't ready yet. I wandered over to the sink to retrieve the potatoes I'd washed and looking out of the window, smiled as I spotted my dad still hard at work in the vegetable patch. He was never happier than when in the garden with a trowel in his hand, and with the weeds growing like crazy and the tomato plants getting a little out of control, I was grateful. A bottle of cider was chilling in the fridge and it was such a pleasant evening it looked like we'd be able to eat outside.

I'd only just started peeling the spuds when the phone rang and wiping my hands on a towel, I reached for the receiver.

'Hey Lou,' I said chirpily as I picked it up.

'Mum says you've been to the Lake District.'

It was an unconventional way of saying hi but that was Lou. 'Yes that's right,' I said.

'What were you doing up there? And why has your mobile been turned off? I couldn't get hold of you. I was worried.'

I answered the first question with, 'On holiday,' and the second by telling her that she was confusing worry with nosiness.

'Did you go with someone?' she asked, the *someone* said in a speculative tone.

'No, I went on my own Lou,' I replied and although she would have loved to hear it, I didn't mention that I'd met someone and when the phone rang I'd hoped it would be him. 'And I had a great time, thanks for asking.'

'Surrounded by all those fields and lakes?'

'Yes I know it's not your sort of thing,' I replied,

identifying her sarcasm and smiling to myself.

'If you wanted to get over Richard you should have gone to France. Who was it who said every woman deserves an affair with a French man? I would even have gone with you.'

'What exactly did mum tell you?' I frowned but Lou ignored the question and surged on.

'I mean who are you going to meet up there? Farmers?'

Shaking my head, I laughed. 'Can we talk about something else for a change? How's Tom?'

'He's fine. So is work. Listen, I think you should try internet dating.'

There was a stunned silence at my end.

'I've read all these articles about it,' she continued. 'It sounds great. Like shopping, but for men not handbags.'

'Lou-'

'Don't say no yet,' she interrupted. 'I think it could perfect for you and I've already found a few hotties.'

'You made me a profile?' I cried.

'No, you can browse for free for a bit. Shall I send you a few photos?'

'Lou stop,' I butted in. 'I'm fine, really. Please stop fussing over me. You may be amazed to hear this but I can survive on my own. I'll meet someone if and when I want to, okay?'

I heard her sigh. 'Fine,' she said. 'But if you're still single at Christmas, I'm introducing you to Paul at the wedding.'

Now I was confused. 'Who the hell's Paul? And since when did you and Tom set the date?'

'Just now,' she said. 'That's what I was ringing to tell you.'

'You could have fooled me,' I squeezed in.

'December nineteenth. Put it in your diary. Paul's that friend of Tom's. He's loaded.'

'Is his bank statement his only asset?' I asked.

'That's for you to find out,' she said and I could imagine her raising her eyebrows suggestively.

'I've got to go Lou,' I sighed, shaking my head. The steamer was starting to rattle like a rocket preparing for take-off.

'Wait, before you do, are you okay with wearing apricot?'

'Apricot?'

'Yeah, as my bridesmaid?'

I hated the colour but it was her day, her decision. 'Sure,' I said.

'Great! And think about what I said.'

'I will. Love you Lou,' I smiled.

'Love you,' she sang.

'What do you think of apricot?' I asked as I negotiated some peas onto my fork.

'They're not really my sort of thing to be honest,' my dad said, his nose wrinkling. 'I much prefer plums.'

'No,' I smiled, 'I meant the colour.'

'Oh,' my dad replied. 'Nice, I guess. Why?' he added, suddenly looking serious. 'You're not thinking of painting out the house in it are you?'

I laughed. 'No, wouldn't dream of it. It's just Lou told me on the phone tonight that she and Tom are getting married at Christmas.'

'Oh,' he said again, his eyebrows shifting in surprise.

'She asked me to wear apricot, as her bridesmaid.'

'You don't like it?' he asked, reading my expression.

I grimaced. 'Do you think I should try and persuade

her otherwise?'

'I think,' he began, holding my gaze, 'that you'll look beautiful no matter what colour your dress is.'

I grinned and my dad returned to slicing his chicken, but there was something else besides the dress that had been bothering me since Lou called.

'What do you think of Tom?' I blurted.

'Tom?' my dad frowned. 'He's a good lad. Why? Don't you think so?'

I started shaking my head. 'I just want to make sure...' I broke off and bit my lip.

'What?' my dad prompted.

'I don't want her to get hurt,' I shrugged. 'I don't want her to make the same mistake I did.'

A sad look crossed my dad's face. 'Hey where's that smile gone? Should I find you a cat?'

I huffed a laugh but it didn't stick around.

'Tom's good for Lou,' he said. 'They're happy aren't they?'

'I thought Richard was right for me,' I replied, 'and so did you, but look what happened there.'

'Actually, I was never that keen on Richard,' my dad admitted.

I frowned. 'What?'

'Well he was okay but...he was never good enough for you.'

'Now you tell me,' I said, finding myself smiling.

'Well I could hardly stop you could I? Just like you'll never persuade Lou to change her mind about apricot... or Tom. They're well suited. I don't think you need to worry.'

I grinned. If my dad was happy then I guessed so was I.

Once I'd waved my dad goodbye I closed the

curtains on the night and sauntered through to the living room where I collapsed into a chair. It had been a long day and now back home, re-immersed in my comfort zone, Dan and the lakes seemed so very far away. Not everyone in the house was quite so relaxed though and when Bea leapt onto my lap, Coco was close behind, feeling playful. Bea skipped across to the arm of the chair, swatting a paw at her sister over her shoulder and then catapulted back to the carpet where Coco rugby tackled her to the ground. Rolling in circles they made little squeaks until Coco, realising she'd bitten off more than she could chew, made a break for it and dashed from the room. Flicks watched them go from her basket near the fireplace and then looked at me and yawned. Beside me, on a stool, sat a pencil and the sketch book I'd bought up north and quietly I reached over and picked it up, Flicks barely twitching an ear as I opened up to a fresh page. Her nose was small and pink, and her ears particularly big. She had a soft white coat speckled with hints of light grey and a shorter than average tail. The basket was lined with a checked blanket and very kindly she stayed perfectly still until I'd finished her portrait.

'What do you think Flicks?' I asked, turning the book around. Standing up she stretched and then wandered over to me and rubbed her nose against the corners. 'That good huh?' I smiled, fussing her head.

I glanced back across at the stool, where the phone sat, and once again my thoughts travelled back to the train station platform I'd stood on earlier that day. We'd had no paper and I'd scribbled my number on the back of Dan's hand, then as the train rumbled into the station he kissed me one last time.

'Harriet?'

I turned back. 'Yes?' I prompted, the rest of his words stuck in his throat.

He swallowed. 'What I said last night...about these last few days being amazing...I meant it.'

Back in my living room the memory reignited the smile his words had incited the first time and then suddenly the phone burst into life.

I picked it up, my heart quickening. 'Hello?'

'Hi, it's me.'

NINE

The first thing I noticed when I pushed the door open and stepped into my shop was the number of little red sold stickers dotted around the room.

'Wow, you've been busy,' I smiled as Charlie appeared out of the office.

'Hey!' she cried. 'Welcome back. How was your trip?'

I walked over to the counter and put down my bag. 'Really great,' I replied, smiling. 'I loved it. And thanks so much for looking after things here. I don't know how I'd manage without you.'

'No problem,' Charlie grinned. 'It's been crazily busy while you were away.'

'So I can see.' There were several gaps dotted along the walls and it was like playing a memory game, trying to guess what was missing. 'The grandfather clock's gone,' I noticed.

'And that bookcase,' Charlie added.

'I should leave you in charge more often,' I beamed.

'There's just one other thing,' Charlie said, her face suddenly more serious.

'What is it?' I asked, preparing myself for bad news.

She fiddled with her necklace, something she only did when she was uneasy. 'Richard called.'

It took a moment for the information to sink in. 'Richard? As in my Richard?'

'Yeah,' she said. 'When I picked up he seemed kind of awkward. He said he'd phoned your house a few times but there was no answer so he thought he'd try the shop.'

'Did he say why he was calling?'

'Well I asked if I could take a message and he just said he wanted to speak to you.'

'He didn't say what about?'

Charlie shook her head.

'Okay, thanks,' I said, biting my lip.

'Do you want a coffee?' she asked. 'I was just going to make one.'

'Sure,' I said a little distractedly. 'I'm just going to nip upstairs but I'll be back in a mo.'

I headed for the staircase.

'Harriet?'

I looked back over my shoulder.

'You okay?' Charlie asked.

'Yeah,' I nodded. 'I'll be right back.'

I only made it to the first floor and slowly I walked over to the window and leant against the wall. It was a cloudy day but the sun was trying to push them aside and down below, on the opposite side of the street, they were setting the chairs and tables up outside the café. The window was full of cakes, cookies and donuts, and I watched as a couple's footsteps faltered as they passed by.

The last time I'd spoken to Richard was the night before he'd left. Everything had seemed normal and I'd fallen asleep beside him with no idea that it was for the last time. He hadn't had the guts to tell me to my face that he was leaving, that he'd found someone else, but now, months later, he called out of the blue. What on earth could he have to say to me, I thought, frowning. I'd hoped my heart had healed but the sick feeling crawling around my stomach made me wonder whether the injury would ever disappear entirely. My medicine up to now had been to think that if he'd never left, I would never have been beside that recycling bin and I would never have found the box of kittens. But now I also had another reason to leave the past in the past, and that reason was Dan.

'So what did you get up to?'

I took the cup of coffee Charlie offered me and perched on a stool across from her.

'A lot of walking, a lot of thinking. It was really refreshing to get away.'

'I think you were quite brave to go by yourself.'

I laughed. 'Really?'

'Yeah, I wouldn't do that.'

'Well actually,' I bit my lip and clasped my mug in both hands, 'I met someone.'

'Someone, as in a guy someone?' Charlie asked, her eyes wide.

I nodded.

'While you were on holiday or before?'

'No, whilst I was there.'

Her smile was as wide as mine. 'What's his name?'

'Dan. He's thirty-two.'

'Cute?'

'Amazing.'

'You got a picture?' she asked excitedly.

I pulled over my bag and turfed out a few things, looking for my phone.

'Here,' I said, handing it over.

'Wow,' she exclaimed, her eyes wide. 'I'm jealous! No wonder you had a good time.'

I laughed.

'Are you going to go back?'

'He promised to visit me here actually.'

'When?'

'I don't know yet. He's got a kid so it has to work round that I guess.'

'A kid? Are you okay with that?'

'I'm still not quite sure what I think to be honest. I didn't ever see myself as a step mum but...he's a great guy. You don't come across them every day. A five year old is an added hurdle but I don't think it's a deal breaker. We all have our histories, right? I mean I come as six for the price of one.'

Charlie grinned. 'I'm happy for you. You deserve it.'

I smiled and looked down at the phone and the picture of us together.

'Hey, what's this?' She'd picked up the copy of Peter Rabbit I'd bought from the second hand book shop.

'Just a souvenir,' I replied and she turned it over in her hands and then opened it up. 'There was this great old bookshop, stacked to the rafters. I was in there for ages-'

'Did you know it's a first edition?' she interrupted, looking at me with wide eyes.

I frowned. 'What?'

'It's a first edition,' she repeated, 'from 1902.'

'How do you know?' I asked, looking from her to the book.

'Greg's mum collects Beatrix Potter books. She knows everything there is to know. She showed me how to spot the older editions although as far as I know she doesn't have anything this special.'

'How special is it?'

'This is one of the very first trade editions,' she said. 'See the end papers?'

I was the antique dealer but suddenly I felt like the apprentice.

'Only a small number were ever printed like this,' Charlie said.

She gave it to me and I ran my fingertips over the board cover, looking at the pictorial inlay of Peter Rabbit in a whole new light. 'What are the chances?' I murmured.

Hearing the doorbell ring I glanced over my shoulder and through the office door.

'No you stay here, finish your coffee,' Charlie said as we both went to stand up. 'I've got this one.'

Five minutes later I was facing the bottom of my coffee cup and although I could have done with another I decided I better get some work done first. A couple of parcels had arrived for me whilst I'd been away and I expected that they were the things I'd ordered online. Car boots weren't the only place I frequented for antique bargains; there were many to be found right at my fingertips. Of course it wasn't the same as seeing them in the flesh and sometimes the photography I had to go by was rather dodgy but there were deals to be found when people emptied their attics and stuck their finds online.

Once in my workshop I opened the first one up and found that it was the group of engravings I'd been the only one to bid on, and as I'd hoped they were fantastic, my smile growing as I laid out all five on the table top. For saying they were several hundred years old I was pleased with the condition they were in. I then turned to the second parcel, cut the tape and lifted the cardboard flaps. I'd bought four old wooden frames and despite a shoddy packing job they were exactly what I'd expected and in the state I'd been promised. At the time I'd bought them I hadn't been exactly sure where they might be used but standing at my desk it was then that I spotted the painting of the lake propped against the wall. The day I'd put it there I was yet to see Lake Windermere but now I recognised it, and looking at the small boat bobbing on the surface of the water, I smiled. Turning it over I bent back the old nails keeping the crude frame in place and then eased the canvas out, the colours of the painting suddenly more vibrant once it had shed the layer of glass on the underside of which clung a film of dust. I reached for the largest of the frames and smiled when it fit to the millimetre. I already knew where I was going to hang it at home.

When I got home my cats were waiting for me. As Coco spotted me open the garden gate, she dropped to the ground on the spot and began rolling around on her back.

'Hello there,' I said, crouching beside her and caressing her head. The others were lounging in the shade of the tree, and hearing my voice they opened their heavy eyes and yawned. 'You've had a tough day then,' I smiled as one by one they pulled themselves up. We walked over to the house, Bea getting distracted on the way by a butterfly, and then stepped into the cool kitchen. 'Dinner is served,' I announced as I placed five food bowls on the tiles, and feeling just as peckish myself I grabbed an apple.

Once changed, I headed back out into the garden and over to the vegetable patch where the strawberries were at last a rich red. I didn't have many strawberry plants but the harvest would be enough for dessert for the next few nights. I crouched down and began picking them off the plant when Modi sat down beside me.

'Hey there fella, you want to help?'

He looked at me, his expression calm, and then meowed. He wanted some company and feeling the same I stroked his head. I remembered in the early days, when Modi and I were still getting to know one another, I'd once read that ginger toms were lively and boisterous, their temperament as vibrant as their markings. But as we sat side by side on the straw, his large yellow eyes patiently watching me place one strawberry after another into the tub, I smiled to myself as I decided that I'd come across more troublesome pigeons. I'd often wondered about Modi's life before he'd come into mine. The vet I'd taken them to see had estimated that they were only six weeks old when I'd found them and I wondered who had been so cold as to separate them from their mother and dump them in a box in the rain. Modi shuffled a little closer, deciding whether to clamber onto my lap when suddenly Bea came tearing across the garden at high speed, startling us both, and disappeared amongst the foliage of the potato plants.

'Hello tiger,' I grinned, spotting a flash of ginger dash through the greenery.

When she leapt back out of her hiding place and pounced on a pebble, I decided to join in. Picking up a lump of dried earth I aimed it a few metres to her right.

The instant it hit the ground, making a little rustle in the grass, she spun round. Her eyes unblinking and every muscle alert and ready, she stared at the spot. Grinning I threw another and she pounced. If she was disappointed that no small creature was hiding in the grass she didn't let on and just continued her game, my knee her next climbing frame with unfortunately all claws still extended.

'Oww Bea,' I cried, easing her off.

Modi looked as pleased as I and when I climbed to my feet and made my way over to the potting table with the tub of strawberries in my hand, he followed. I wanted to start off some haricots for an autumn harvest and uncovering a plastic tray ideal enough, I filled it with compost and then dotted around the seeds, sprinkling on a last layer of compost to cover them. Modi had watched me do this sitting on the table top beside me but sensing I'd finished he strolled over and put his two fronts paws up on my chest.

'All right little guy, I get the idea,' I said, sweeping him up into my arms, and he nuzzled against my face as I held him close.

The love I felt for him ran deep, right to my very core, and I wondered, as I had done so more than once before, whether it was possible to love anything more. I would never forget the day I had first held him in my arms. It had changed me. Suddenly, for the first time, I had not one but five dependants. So young and delicate, I was their sole protector and as they'd grown I'd been there to help and guide, like a parent to a child. That would never change. If anything my love for them grew with every hurdle and I knew as I closed my eyes, feeling the rise and fall of Modi's chest against mine, that my love was returned.

When dusk fell at the end of each day it was not uncommon for Modi to wander off for a couple of hours. Whilst the girls seemed content to stay close to home, Modi would cross the garden, squeeze through a gap in the hedge and head for the fields. Hunting was the height of feline entertainment. Sometimes I would see him, out of the bathroom window, sitting in the long grass often for long stretches at a time, just waiting for that moment a mouse appeared, and then like a spring he would pounce. He'd return having collected all sorts of things in his fur, from leaves to sticky pods and grass seed, and then he would sit patiently as I brushed them out. Sometimes I began to wonder whether he did it on purpose.

'Have fun,' I called as I watched him weave between the flowers and then disappear. 'And don't go near the road.'

Hearing a huff I looked to my left and sure enough, Mrs Ellis was standing in her garden, muttering under her breath. I didn't want to know what she was saying, I could all too easily imagine it went along the lines of; *foolish girl shouldn't have let her husband run away. Then again she's clearly insane, talking to her cats like that, so of course he left.* She shot me glances of the same calibre each day and although my skin wasn't that thick, I tried my best to deflect the blows.

'Good evening,' I called with a smile. She may have been rude but she would not draw me into a battle of wills. I would be polite even if she found it a bore.

'Your cats have been in my garden again,' she frowned back. 'Why can't you control them?'

I cleared my throat and wondered as I glanced at the low wall separating our properties whether she had asked the question rhetorically. She had made it perfectly clear more than once before that she didn't like cats but surely she understood that I couldn't stop them hopping over the wall. It wasn't until then that I noticed that Mona was wandering in her flowerbed but before I could call her over, Mrs Ellis reached for a broom.

'I'm so sorry,' I apologised, but failed to mean the words as my neighbour angrily swotted at Mona who fled the scene in terror.

'They're such a nuisance,' Mrs Ellis mumbled once content she had disinfected the area.

So was she I thought to myself, feeling my anger build, but I bit my tongue. An outburst, no matter how much she enjoyed provoking me, would do no good in the long run and unfortunately I knew that this would not be the last time we had this conversation.

TEN

'What do you think fellas?'

I took a couple of steps back and leant against the garden wall where Flicks and Coco were perched side by side, and admired my new car.

'Nice huh?'

Bea was the only one intrigued enough to get a closer look and reaching the wheel she gave it a sniff. I'd at last taken the plunge. After hours and hours of trawling through newspapers and websites, at last I had wheels again. Shopping for cars was considerably less fun that shopping for antiques, there was so much more than appearances to take into account, but nevertheless I had a smile on my face now.

'Hello there Harriet,' Mr Ellis said as he stepped out of his front door. 'I see you've got your car back.'

'Actually,' I smiled, 'it's a different one.'

'Really? It looks just the same.'

And he was right. I'd been considering something different, a little newer, or at least my mum had tried to persuade me to get a little more up to date, but in the end I'd followed my heart, as I so often did.

'Yeah, it's very similar to my last one, same colour too,' I told Eddie. 'I just like these old CVs. They've got character.'

Eddie chuckled. 'I think your little cat likes it.'

Bea now had her two front paws up on the bumper as though looking for a way to climb onto the bonnet.

'She's a tinker this one,' I grinned, picking her up.

'I had a cat as a young lad,' Eddie said. 'Archie his name was. Looked a lot like this one,' he smiled, nodding at Bea.

She looked back at the old man with wide curious eyes as he reached out to stroke her, unsure whether to recoil or purr.

'You are a sweetie,' he grinned and as he began tickling her under the chin she opted for the latter. 'I never had any brothers or sisters,' Eddie carried on, 'and so Archie was my play mate. We did everything together.' The skin round his eyes crinkled as a gentle smile crossed his face. 'He was a great friend.'

I could imagine that boy and his cat and wondered if they were tears in Eddie's eyes as for a moment he looked away. 'Aren't you tempted to have another?' I asked.

'I would, I've always liked cats, but Margaret's not so keen,' he said, shaking his head.

Why didn't that surprise me, I thought to myself.

'You've done well with these five Harriet,' he announced, his smile reappearing. 'They're lucky to have you caring for them.'

'I'm as lucky to have them,' I admitted.

I'd got my car in time for the Sunday flea market and

set off early in the morning feeling optimistic about the hunt ahead. It had been a good few weeks since I'd been to one and I needed to replenish stock as well as my appetite. As I approached the makeshift car park situated in a field, the traffic got thicker, men in florescent jackets trying to organise the chaos, and eventually I was in and parked up. The stalls were still a couple of hundred metres away and it would be quite a walk back if laden with purchases but it was not uncommon for me to make several trips back to the car during one spree. My purse heavy with change, I slung my bag over my shoulder and set off.

In the days when Richard came with me, he would get impatient as I took my time looking closely at every stall, but if you didn't you missed things. Sometimes the greatest finds were buried in the bottom of boxes under heaps of old toys or sitting beneath an old video player or behind a stack of DVDs. He'd wander on ahead with itchy feet only to be called back when I spotted something and needed help to carry it. These days I had to make do with just two hands.

I was only a couple of stalls in when something caught my eye. Rolled up under the table was a Persian rug, perhaps antique, and crouching down I went to investigate whether it was as promising as it first looked. I pulled back the corner, hoping to be delighted, but instantly the anticipation was squandered. It was nothing but a modern reproduction of those I sought and I stood back up.

'You can unroll it if you like,' said the stall owner with a large smile, thinking he could smell a sale.

'No, that's okay,' I replied politely. He shuffled round his stall and unravelled it all the same, a cloud of dust billowing into the air as he did so. I could feel his eyes burning into the back of my head as I swiftly moved on.

A bit further down I stopped face to face with a teddy bear. He was sitting amongst a heap of soft toys and dolls but this one, with his hand stitched nose and glass eyes, was special. I picked him up and gave his tummy a small squeeze, feeling an old growler beneath the golden mohair. Although I wasn't sure of the make without a little more research, he was undoubtedly a sought after antique bear.

'How much for this?' I asked the woman behind the stall.

Unfortunately for me she knew its worth as well as I did. I put the bear back down feeling disappointed but as my gaze wandered further down the table I spotted a plastic bag full of cutlery. I stepped up to it and picked out a piece at random, subtly looking for hallmarks. As I'd hoped it was silver and remarkably untarnished despite its clear lack of care. In the bag there must have been a full dinner set for twelve; knives, forks, spoons, the lot. I looked over at the woman again, wondering whether it was worth asking the price. Yet surely if she knew what she had she wouldn't just sling it all in a plastic bag?

'Excuse me?' I said again. 'How much for these?'

'A tenner and they're yours,' she shrugged.

I couldn't believe my luck but did my best not to seem overly pleased and calmly handed over the money before picking up the bag. I'd expected it to weigh a fair bit but it was even heavier than I'd imagined and I walked away looking forward to sorting through them later.

I found the vast breadth of people who attended car boots and flea markets an interesting lot and those behind the stalls just as curious. I passed people from all walks of life strolling up and down fields each Sunday, sometimes I even recognised one or two regulars. From young couples to elderly women with little dogs, teenage girls to families with kids, everyone was hunting for different things. Many walked away with nothing, others with a new lamp or a couple of books. There was one old man I saw every time, hobbling from stall to stall with the aid of his walking stick asking if anyone had any stamps, and today was no exception. The stall at which we crossed paths replied yes to his question and with a smile he propped his walking stick against the table and began sifting through the old tin they gave him. I carried on to the next table where a tall man with a penchant for tattoos was selling some old monogrammed bed linen. The sight was a peculiar one, almost as though he was watching the stall for his elderly mother.

'Hello,' he said softly as I took a closer look. Far from intimidating he was only too pleased to help me unfold a few so that I could properly check their condition. I bought a couple as well as a basket, haggling over the price for all three until we were both happy.

By the time I returned to the car I had my arms full and considered the last couple of hours well spent. The best find was an antique chopping board, over two inches thick and incredibly heavy. It had been so well used over the years that there was a hollow in the middle and the wood was smooth beneath my fingertips. Perhaps I'd keep it for myself, I thought as I put it in the boot, seduced by its patina.

I pulled the car keys from my bag and started the engine. I'd not managed to get the radio working yet so reaching over I pressed a few more buttons until suddenly it burst into life.

'That's better,' I murmured. I began flicking through the stations but hadn't got far when I came across a song I'd first heard years ago, rumbling from our garage. Back then band practice was always Saturday afternoons and for hours on end Ollie and his mates would play their set again and again until they'd reached perfection. Hearing it now on the radio was still a strange thing and I smiled as I put the car into gear. I would call him when I got home, I decided. It would be good to hear how he was getting on.

The call went straight to voicemail. I dialled Ollie's number a second time but again a woman's voice told me to leave a message.

'Hey Ollie, it's me, Harriet. I just thought I'd see how everything was going but I'll call you another time okay? All right, well, speak soon. Bye.'

I put the phone back down on the kitchen table and wandered over to the kettle which had almost finished boiling. As I made a cup of tea I couldn't help but think about my brother's last visit. We'd had fun but then after the phone call at Sunday lunchtime his mood had fallen like the temperature at winter's first frost. I hadn't spoken to him since that day and suddenly I felt guilty, wondering if he needed me, but then frowning I told myself that I was being silly. What rock star wants their big sister ringing them all the time, asking if they're feeling okay? He was probably working; shooting a video, writing songs or just recovering from a gig last night. He was fine and he'd call back when he was ready. He knew where to find me.

I knew the tea would still be too hot but I cautiously

took a sip anyway and as Mona saw me sit down and pat my knee, she came straight over and jumped up onto my lap.

'I don't have any biscuits,' I warned her as she began sniffing the edge of the table, but it seemed, as she turned in little circles and then settled into a ball, that for once her mind was not on food and she was simply happy to be with me. She purred as I stroked her soft head, the steady rhythm of my fingers tracing a line from the top of her nose to the base of her skull soothing us both, and I found my thoughts wandering back to the Lake District and Dan, as they so often did. I hated to wish time away but I longed to see him again and with every day that passed, our time together seemed more and more like a distant dream.

I jumped as abruptly the phone started ringing and Mona looked up at me as though wondering why her sleep had been disturbed. Ollie must have got my message already I thought, or perhaps it was Dan.

'Hello,' I said.

'Harriet, it's me.'

Instantly my smile vanished. For so long I had wanted to hear the voice on the end of the line, the voice which had haunted my thoughts and my dreams, say my name and as I closed my eyes he did so again.

'Harriet? Are you there?'

I licked my lips and tasted tears. 'Richard,' I eventually stumbled, and although I tried to keep the emotion from my voice I had no doubt that he could hear it.

'Please don't hang up,' he said and I found myself wondering why I hadn't already. But of course I already knew the answer; I still loved him, despite how deeply he'd hurt me. My hand holding the phone was trembling and the whole scope of reasons why he'd want to talk to me now raced through my mind in a tenth of a second. Maybe he was sorry. Maybe he had finished with Sophie. Maybe he had realised his mistake and wanted me back. Immediately my mind pushed all thoughts of Dan aside and a surge of pain split my chest. I put a hand over my mouth as I choked on the lump in my throat.

'I've been trying to call you,' he said. 'I want to speak to you.'

'What do you want?' I managed to muster.

I could almost imagine his downcast eyes as he didn't reply straight away. 'I was wondering how you were,' he said gently.

I shook my head. *How I was?* I felt sick. I felt broken. I'd thought I was moving on but he'd cruelly come back, reopened the wound, and now I was hurting, as much as ever before. 'I don't think you have a right to know anymore,' I replied.

There was a long pause and then he said, 'I guess you're right. But I want you to know that I'm sorry Harriet. I should never have left like that. I know now that it was wrong.'

My heart jolted. Was this the moment I had been waiting for? The one I'd imagined time and again. I couldn't breathe as I waited for him to say that he had left her and wanted me back, but it never came.

'Listen, have you seen my guitar?'

My jaw dropped and a strange sort of laugh left my lips.

'Your guitar? Is that what you are really ringing about?' I could hear the distain in my voice and roughly wiped the tears from my face, angry that I'd spilt them for him.

'I thought I might have left it there,' he said.

'Well you didn't,' I replied bluntly.

'Are you sure?'

'I think I would have noticed if your guitar was hanging around. I could hardly miss it could I?'

He was quiet, like a scolded child, and I'd had enough.

'I have to go,' I said.

'Hattie?'

I didn't respond.

'I know you hate me and I expect you don't much care what I think anymore...but I hope you're okay.'

He waited for me to say something and I closed my eyes, trying to dam the fresh flood of tears. And then the line went dead.

ELEVEN

'How do I look?' I asked Coco.

My little spotty cat stared at me for a whole half a second before returning to her grooming and I looked back at the mirror, taking a deep breath as I straightened out my dress. Dan would be here any moment and my heart was pounding. On my bed was the heap of outfits I had tried and discarded but at last I had settled on the dress which had started out as first choice. I turned to the side, making sure one last time that I was happy, and then stared myself sternly in the eyes and told myself I looked good. Hearing tyres pull up outside the gate, I glanced out of the window; it was him. Quickly I shoved the other clothes back into the wardrobe and then dashed downstairs, pulling the door open before Dan had even reached out to knock on it.

'Hey,' he said as our eyes met.

I had waited impatiently almost two long weeks for this day and now he was here I felt dizzy with a mixture of nerves and excitement. If his stomach was swirling with butterflies like mine, he didn't let it show.

'Hi,' I smiled.

'These are for you,' he said, looking down at the bouquet of flowers in his hand. 'Although having just walked through your garden, they suddenly look a little pathetic,' he laughed.

'Don't be silly,' I grinned, taking them. 'They're beautiful.'

'Perhaps I should have brought chocolates. I know you said you liked gardening but I wasn't expecting a miniature Sissinghurst.'

I didn't know what to say and so just smiled again.

'You know,' he said, taking a step forward, 'I haven't been able to get you out of my head since you left.'

His eyes flickered searchingly across my face and reaching out he sought for my hand. I gazed at his lips, remembering how they had kissed me, and then looked deep into his eyes as he pulled me closer until I heard a splash from somewhere over the neighbour's wall. My attention travelled past his shoulder and found Mrs Ellis who having once thrown out a bucket of water, realised there was something happening next door worth spying on. She stared at us from beneath large pinched brows, no doubt making note of the flowers and our proximity, and I looked back at Dan with a smile.

'Let's go inside.'

When I opened my eyes the next morning I found myself nose to nose with a furry ginger ball. Propping myself up on one elbow I realised it was Modi and he had neatly curled himself up on the pillow between Dan and I.

'What are you doing in here?' I hissed at him, lines

on my brow. He wasn't allowed in the bedroom and he knew it, and waking up he looked back at me with large innocent eyes. 'You're a tinker,' I told him, looking towards the door and noticing it was ajar. Dan was still asleep and I was certain he wouldn't appreciate waking up to find three of us in the bed. Modi looked confused as, first I peeled away the covers and then went to pick him up, and deciding he didn't want to go anywhere, he dug in his claws so that if he was ousted it meant the pillow was going with him.

'Fine, how about some breakfast?' I whispered, realising he wasn't going to shift unwillingly otherwise. 'Do you want some biscuits?' Modi knew what I meant and instantly he was wide awake and trotted with me across the room and out of the door.

'There you go,' I told him as once in the kitchen I offered him a bowl. He made a small meow and then started eating and feeling my frown disappear, I stroked his head. 'It's impossible to stay angry with you,' I admitted, laughing at myself.

Gooseflesh on my bare skin, I went back upstairs and climbed into bed, pulling the covers up to my neck as I snuggled against Dan's back. I lightly traced my fingertips over his shoulder blades as I listened to the steady rhythm of his breathing, and then when he stirred I heard him murmur, 'You're cold.'

'Morning,' I whispered as he rolled over.

'Morning,' he smiled as his dark eyes found mine. He pulled me close, enveloping me in his body heat and I nestled against his chest, my head tucked beneath his chin.

'You okay?' he asked, his words still slurred with sleep.

I nodded but closing my eyes knew that *okay* far

from covered what I felt. I was happier than I think I'd ever been. And I was in love, as he was and had told me so twelve hours ago as we lay outside on the grass, the night air warm and the dark sky twinkling with an eternity of stars. It was still hard to believe that it was real and happening to me, when I'd given up on love, and suddenly I felt like I needed some reassurance that it hadn't all been just a dream.

Dan lifted my chin with his finger so that he could look me in the eyes. 'Yes, I love you Hattie.'

I placed my hand on Dan's chest and as I felt his heart beat against my palm I remembered that I was not the only one who had been hurt in the past. He put his hand on top of mine.

'It's yours now. I know you won't break it.'

I leant forwards and kissed him. 'I won't break it,' I whispered.

We skipped breakfast and eventually sidled out from beneath the sheets as the village church bells chimed midday.

'There's only one thing missing from the picture you painted of this place,' Dan said as I reached for two mugs. 'Well five.'

I knew exactly what he was talking about and grinned.

'I haven't seen one cat yet.'

'But they've seen you,' I smiled. I pointed across to the window and Dan's gaze followed. Bea was sitting on the exterior sill, staring at us through the window with narrow, suspicious eyes. 'And over there,' I added, nodding towards the shoe rack where Flicks was sniffing Dan's boot laces.

'We're surrounded,' Dan whispered jokily.

'I'm afraid they're a bit shy of strangers so they're keeping their distance.'

'Who's that over there?' he asked, looking towards the doorway.

Modi was peering around the frame, looking from me to Dan and then back to me. 'That's Modi,' I replied.

'Ah, the man of the house,' Dan said. He stood up and began walking over as though to introduce himself and my thoughts travelled back to the cat who had been sitting on top of the post box when Dan and I had first met. He had disappeared when Dan came too close and from the look on Modi's face, he was about to do the same.

'It's okay Modi,' I told him and instantly he sought me out with his wide yellow eyes. 'It's okay,' I repeated gently. Modi looked back at the figure stalking towards him and then darted through his legs and made straight for me.

Dan laughed as he watched him go. 'Not a good start,' he admitted as Modi hid behind my legs.

I smiled and gave Modi a reassuring tickle. 'He'll get used to you.' The phone started ringing from the living room. 'Back in a minute,' I said.

I picked up the receiver as my gaze fell on an empty wine bottle across the room. Somewhere there were two glasses as well and a smile crept across my face as I remembered last night and simultaneously said, 'Hello?'

'Hattie? Is that you?'

'Hey Lou, yeah it's me.'

There was a pause at my sister's end and then she said, 'Have you adopted another cat or something?'

I frowned. 'What? Why?'

'You sound different.'

'Different?' I repeated.

'Happier, I think.'

I peered back through the doorway into the kitchen, smiling as I spotted Dan kneeling down, his hand outstretched towards Modi. 'I'm having a good day,' I told her. 'But no, I haven't adopted another cat.'

'A puppy then?'

I laughed. 'No. I'm just enjoying the summer.'

'That sounds awfully suspicious,' she said, 'especially considering the weather.' I looked across at the window and noticed it was dull outside, and pinched the bridge of my nose between finger and thumb. I'd slipped up there.

'I rang your shop first, expected you to be there,' she said.

'No, I'm taking the weekend off.'

'So Charlie said.'

'Did you call about something particular Lou?' I asked, trying to change the course of the conversation although it was undoubtedly too late. As soon as she was finished here I was certain she'd be making further enquiries about me and my recent activity elsewhere.

'Yes actually,' she replied, suddenly matter of fact. 'You know it's mum's sixtieth soon right? Well I was thinking how about we put on a surprise party.'

My lips twisted into a frown. I wasn't so sure that was a good idea. 'That's sweet Lou but I don't think she wants to be reminded it's her birthday, never mind celebrate it,' I said.

'Don't be silly. It'll be great. We'll have it at my place. I'll organise everything, you just bring them down.' She sounded excited and I rubbed my face, wishing I was still in bed.

'Have you mentioned this to anyone else?' I asked.

'Everyone,' she confirmed.

'Even Ollie?'

'Well not Ollie, I couldn't reach him, but everyone else thinks it's a good idea.'

But they weren't here. They didn't see their parents on a regular basis like I did and Mum was growing grouchier by the day. If anything she could do with a holiday but I'd already tried suggesting that.

'I'm not sure Lou,' I said. 'Mum seems kind of down recently.'

'Then this is just what she needs,' she replied brightly.

I could hear Dan rummaging through the cupboards looking for the coffee and decided I didn't care. 'Fine, as long as you arrange it.'

'Okay, great. Well, I'll leave you to whatever it is you don't want to share with me.'

'Bye Lou,' I said, determined not to fall into her guilt trap. Dan would be mine, and only mine, for a little while longer yet, or so I'd hoped.

The sun was beginning to show its face through a nick in the clouds as we took my favourite path out of the village, the one I walked almost every week but never tired of. It began up in the fields, with views across the undulating hills, the dull ring of cattle bells carried by the wind. Then the path took us into the forest, the undergrowth rustling with secrets, and eventually into a valley through which ran a gentle river. Tall, curious limestone formations towered out of the trees and trout splashed in the water as we followed the riverside path. We crossed it by a narrow wooden bridge, the surface green with lichen, and once on the other side Dan stopped me in my tracks.

'Look,' he whispered. A deer was standing on the

path ahead, her delicate figure framed by the oaks whose thick branches spread far. She stared at us, unsure of our intentions and we stared back, admiring such a rare sight.

'If only you had your camera,' I whispered.

'Yes,' he replied softly. 'Although sometimes I think it's better to look for real than through a lens.'

When she decided to leave, we watched her deep red coat melt into the colours of the forest, and I reached for Dan's hand. I had never seen a deer here before and although I didn't believe in such things, I found myself wondering if she was a good omen. It felt good walking the paths I knew so well with another's footsteps beside mine, my thoughts voiced aloud rather than left to circle my mind, and when the sky fell dark and an unexpected shower forced us home early, the rain seeping down our necks and creeping through our layers until it reached our skin, I did not complain.

'Let's eat out tonight,' Dan said as he pulled a dry t-shirt over his head.

Still beneath the bed sheet, I returned his warm smile. 'Okay. I'll just get dressed.'

'Wow,' was all he could say when shortly afterwards I walked downstairs in my favourite little black dress. I blushed and brushed the hair from my face. I hadn't had that kind of reaction for some time and, looking back at him, I was thinking the same thing.

The restaurant was almost full as we were lead to a small table tucked in the corner of the room and once a young waitress had vigorously written down our order in large round font, she zigzagged her way back to the kitchen.

'It's nice here,' Dan smiled, looking around.

'Well I hope the food's as good as it smells,' I said. 'I've never actually been here before.'

He took a swig of his beer. 'It feels a long time since I was a pot washer. God, I hated that job. The chef was a nightmare.'

I laughed. 'My sister in law is a chef.'

'You don't like her?' he asked, reading my expression.

'Neither would you if you met her,' I assured him.

'I wonder if it's part of their training,' Dan mused, 'learning how to be hard work.'

'Well I think Karen was born with that know-how,' I said raising my eyebrows. 'I don't know how Ryan sticks her.'

'Is he an older or younger brother?'

'Older,' I said. 'Although not the eldest.'

'Tell me about them,' Dan asked. 'Your siblings.'

I made a small laugh. 'Where do I start? Well Will's the oldest. He's fun but he can be difficult. He works in London, in advertising, and he is well known for being a ladies man. I'm telling you he puts Casanova in the shade.'

Dan laughed.

'Then there's Ryan,' I said. 'Married to the aforementioned Karen. He's an architect and really loves his work.'

'Do they have any kids?' Dan asked.

'No, although they're currently looking for a bigger place, somewhere in the country. God I hope he knows what he's doing,' I grimaced. 'After me there's my sister Louise,' I continued. 'She's really creative... and nosy,' I added, grinning. 'She lives south a bit with her fiancé Tom; they're getting married at Christmas. Chris is number five. He's a writer, journalism that is. He's a quiet sort, easy going. And then Ollie of course is the drummer.'

'Of course,' Dan repeated. 'The famous drummer.'

'He was always so driven by his music as a kid.'

'Are you close?' Dan asked. 'With them all?'

'We were,' I replied. 'I was closer with my sister than any friend at school and I looked out for my little brothers like I was their second mother.'

Dan smiled at that.

'But then one by one we left home,' I carried on. 'There were lesser chairs around the dinner table, fewer people to share the birthday cakes. When I moved out I didn't go far but the others chased their dreams elsewhere. Before I knew it, I was the only one left here. They visit when they can, as do I in return. We talk on the phone of course, but I guess it is different now. I don't know if we can call ourselves close,' I said, 'but I like to think so.'

'You sound a varied bunch,' Dan commented after a moment's thought. 'I sometimes think I missed out.'

To be an only child was a strange concept for me and although sometimes growing up I had thought it would be nice to have my own bedroom or a little more privacy, the truth was if there was ever a component missing, it just didn't feel right.

'Tell me about your mum,' I asked Dan.

'My mum? Well for a start she'd be jealous of yours. She had always wanted a large family but couldn't have kids. So she adopted me,' he said, 'and found out I was more than enough trouble to be getting on with.'

I grinned. 'I bet.'

'She's a cheerful woman. Makes the best mince pies at Christmas,' he added. 'She's a great listener. She likes gardening too,' he said, smiling at me. 'And she has a cat.'

I laughed. It seemed there were a few things we had in common.

Once we'd eaten the main course I went to the bathroom. Staring into the mirror above the sink I made sure everything, from my hair to my neckline, was just so and then turned for the door at the same moment it was pushed open from the other side and a very familiar face walked in.

'Harriet? Wow, what a pleasant surprise!' It was Sian but the look on her face was more consistent with the surprised rather than pleasant part of her claim.

'Hi,' I said, smiling politely. 'How are you?'

'Good, good,' she nodded, clinging to her bag strap and changing her weight from one boot to the other. 'Just out with the girls.'

'Oh right,' I said, wondering if I should be miffed that I hadn't been invited, regardless of whether I would have wanted to go or not. 'How's Steven?' I asked, thankful I could recall her fiancé's name.

'He's great.'

There was a pause.

'It's nice here isn't it?' I said.

'Um very,' she agreed.

I wasn't sure but Sian seemed to be acting a bit unusual. It wasn't like her to avoid conversation, in fact she wasn't trying at all. She answered every question as simply as possible and then had none of her own, and slowly she was beginning to sidle around me towards the cubicles.

'Okay, well I'll see you around then,' I smiled, getting the idea.

'Yeah,' she nodded with sincerity as faux as the fur trim on her boots.

I left the toilets wanting to double back to the mirror to check that their wasn't a big sign on my forehead screaming, *warning, don't get too close*, but whilst returning to my seat a squawk of laughter drew my attention to an animated table and suddenly all became clear. Sitting around the corner with sparkling rosé in their glasses was Sian's girlie group and amongst the faces were a few familiar ones including Sophie, the woman who had once been my best friend, my bridesmaid, and then slept with my husband. I froze in my tracks, my gaze transfixed, and slowly the laughter died away as one by one they realised who was looking on.

'You okay?' Dan frowned as I hurried back to our table and asked if he was ready to leave.

'Yeah, well no,' I stumbled. 'Can we go?'

'Sure,' he frowned. 'If you want to.' It wasn't until we were back in the car and halfway home that he asked me why.

'Ghosts from my past,' I said simply.

'Do you want to talk about it?'

I wasn't sure but even if I did I couldn't help but think that talking about it with Dan would surely only create more problems than it solved.

'Cats remind me of my granddad,' Dan said as he handed me a cup of tea. He sat down beside me on the sofa and nodded over at Bea who was fast asleep perched on top of a stack of books. 'They fall asleep anywhere, anytime. Just like he used to.'

I smiled, just like I suspected he'd hoped, and he put his hand on top of mine.

'I'm sorry about that, about back there,' I fumbled, shaking my head and knowing he deserved some sort of explanation.

'It doesn't matter,' he replied. 'Are you all right?'

I inhaled deeply. 'Yeah, I'm okay.' I knew where the conversation was headed and I could do nothing to change its course. I looked down into my mug, unable to meet his eyes as they searched my face.

'Hattie?' he said, his fingers tightening a little around my hand. 'How long were you married?'

My throat thickening, I put my mug down without taking a sip. 'Almost four years.'

'And was that him you saw back there?'

'No,' I replied, ever so slightly shaking my head. 'It was the woman he left me for. Sophie.'

'You know her?' he asked.

'Yes,' I nodded. 'She was my best friend once. Richard told me in a letter that he wasn't coming back. He didn't say that he'd met someone else but it didn't take long for word to get around. I felt like such an idiot.'

I looked away, feeling awkward about my pain.

'Joe was two when my wife Claire told me we weren't happy,' Dan said. 'It was news to me. I had been happy. But out of the blue she told me she wanted a divorce.'

I turned my head and looked at him.

'I know it hurts,' he said, 'and I think that's why you went to the Lake District, isn't it?' he asked. 'That's what you were talking about when you said you needed to get away?'

I nodded.

A small smile crossed his face and he said, 'In that case would it be bad to say I'm glad?'

I spluttered a small laugh.

'I'm serious. If none of that had happened I wouldn't be here with you right now.'

At that moment Modi appeared and rubbed himself against my leg as though to remind me that if none of it had happened he wouldn't be here with me either. I brushed the tears from my cheeks and Dan folded his arms around me.

'I swear I won't ever hurt you like that Hattie.'

'I know.' I reached out and stroked Modi between the ears. 'I know.'

TWELVE

The early August sunshine was streaming through the bedroom curtains and outside the window the birds were chattering excitably. Curled up beside Dan, I smiled as he kissed the back of my neck but when I heard a small scratch at the door I knew that our Sunday morning lie-in wouldn't last much longer. Gradually the scratching became more persistent and then, as I propped myself up on one elbow, Mona started meowing.

'She won't stop until she's been fed,' I told Dan as I made to get out of bed, his hands reluctant to let me go.

'So what's the plan today?' he asked, sitting up as I pulled on a dressing gown.

'I don't know, what do you want to do?'

'I thought Sunday was car boot day,' he said.

I looked back at him. 'You want to go to a car boot?' I asked, frowning.

'Yeah, course,' he replied. 'Why do you look so surprised?'

'Well you might find it boring. It's mostly just rubbish.'

'But if you sift through the rubbish you can find all sorts of things, you once told me. Come on, I want you to teach me what to look for. I can help carry if nothing else.'

I laughed. 'Okay, sure. If you really want.' I opened the bedroom door and Mona burst in.

'Who would have thought that such a small thing could make so much noise,' Dan said, looking at her.

'Why do you think I called her Mona?' I smiled. 'We'll meet you downstairs.'

I turned on the toaster and gazed out of the kitchen window. Mrs Ellis was in her front garden, hanging out a string of clean washing, and unaware that I could see her she kept casting suspicious glances at my house in between the various garments. With the sun out, she had exchanged her usual attire for a floral dress which I suspected had been at the back of her wardrobe for a good twenty years, the tired fabric gaping at the buttons. Her hair was scraped into a severe bun which did nothing to soften her hard features and her brow was as creased as the pillowcase she was pegging on the line. No doubt she was beginning to wonder who the stranger was staying with me and her nosiness getting the better of her, she ventured over to the wall separating my garden from hers and hovered beside the bins, pretending to be busy.

'I've put some toast in,' I told Dan as he walked into the kitchen.

'Strawberry jam?' he said, opening the fridge.

'Yeah, sure.'

'Do you want to eat outside?' he asked as he walked over, his hands falling to my waist.

'As long as you don't mind being spied on,' I told him.

He frowned and then followed my gaze out of the window.

'That's Mrs Ellis,' I informed him.

'She looks formidable,' he commented.

'She is, believe me.'

He spread the jam on the toast and then whisked up the plate.

'Wait, where are you going?' I asked as he headed for the door.

'The garden,' he said casually.

My heart sank at the prospect of a battle with Mrs Ellis and I followed reluctantly with the coffee.

As we stepped out into the sunshine Mrs Ellis disappeared behind the dustbins, making more noise than necessary in order to keep up her guise that she was in fact busy and not spying.

'Morning,' Dan smiled as she reappeared.

'Hello,' I said as well. I sat down and dared another glance in her direction as she managed a hello. She wanted to frown but her eyes on Dan, a small smile was creeping through the cracks of her well-honed disapproving glare.

'Lovely day isn't it?' Dan said to her.

My eyebrows shot upwards as Mrs Ellis failed to control the smile and suddenly she looked ten years younger as the serious lines disappeared from her face.

'Yes, it is love,' she replied.

I looked at Dan as she walked back to her front door and then disappeared inside, with a grin. 'I think she fancies you.'

Dan laughed.

'You do realise that means she'll hate me even more

135

now?' I told him.

'She doesn't hate you Hattie. There's nothing to hate about you.'

I smiled at him over the rim of my coffee cup.

'Come on, let's eat up,' he said. 'I don't want to miss all the bargains.'

'What about that?' Dan said, pointing at an old lamp.

'Um...' I said, struggling to tell him outright that he'd picked out probably the most horrendous thing on the stall. 'Do you really like it?' I asked him.

'Well, it's kind of vintage looking isn't it? Don't you like it?'

When I didn't say anything he laughed.

'Ah, so that's why you didn't barter harder for that chair back there either.'

'I'm sorry Dan,' I admitted, grinning, 'but it was just...ugly.'

'Maybe, but it was old,' he tried in his defence.

'I'm afraid it wasn't as old as you think it was.'

'It wasn't?' he frowned. 'The bloke told me it was eighteenth century.'

'Well then he didn't know how old it was either,' I said with a consolatory smile.

'I'm not a very useful apprentice am I?' Dan mused as we carried on walking.

'Don't be silly,' I told him, nudging him on the arm. 'I would never have got that fireback back to the car on my own.'

'I didn't think I was going to make it at one point,' he laughed. 'It was heavier than it looked.'

'And I thought I'd bagged a tough guy,' I teased.

He smiled and reached for my hand. 'You'll never guess what I saw back there?'

I raised an eyebrow and waited for him to tell me.

'A broken step ladder. Why on earth would someone try and sell that?'

I laughed. 'I think the worst I've ever seen is an old toilet seat.'

Dan shook his head. 'That's just weird.'

'Like I warned you,' I grinned, 'it's not all good stuff and sometimes you have to look hard.'

I stopped to look in a box full of books.

'I'll be back in a minute,' I heard Dan say and when he did he had grin on his face. 'I think I've found something, something good this time.'

'Oh yeah?' I smiled.

He led me over to the stall opposite and pointed at an old gramophone. 'Look. The bloke says it still works.'

It sat on a plastic sheet lying on the ground, surrounded by a strange assortment of other things, and smiling I tiptoed over.

'So, how did I do?' Dan asked as I reached out and touched the horn.

'I love it,' I said, looking back at him.

The elderly man who owned the stall came over and considering his appearance and what else he had for sale, I tried to gage whether a bargain could be struck.

'Tell you what, I'll throw in that box of records too,' he said as I mulled it over.

'Deal,' I smiled.

When we got back home, the first thing Dan did was try it out. Picking one of the discs at random he put it on and then lowered the needle. At first it crackled and then he looked over at me, grinning, as the music began, upbeat and reminiscent of the fifties.

'May I have this dance?' he said, offering me his

hand.

I laughed and took a step towards him, my smile growing as he pulled me close and we started dancing around the kitchen, the tiles cool beneath my bare feet as we span in fast circles. I don't know how long we danced for and how long it was that we lay in each other's arms afterwards but I knew, like Cinderella, that the magic would eventually come to an end.

Modi jumped up and put his front paws on my knee. It was his way of telling me that he wanted holding and bending down I scooped him up.

'Happy?' I asked him as he leant against me, his chin propped on my shoulder.

His purring was a sufficient response and I smiled, stroking his back.

'You get heavier every time,' I whispered to him.

'Harriet?'

I heard Dan call my name and looked back over my shoulder, smiling as I saw a camera pointed my way. The shutter clicked and that moment, with Modi's heart so close to mine, was captured forever. But my smile soon faded. Dan put down the camera on top of his bag, which was packed and sitting just outside the front door. Seeing my face fall he stepped up to me and I encouraged Modi down.

'I wish I wasn't going so soon,' he said.

I nodded and, finding it hard to look at him, my gaze fell to the ground.

He reached for my hand and held it tightly in his. 'Will you come back to the Lake District? Will you come visit me again?'

'Of course,' I said, inwardly fighting with tears.

He reached for my face and stroked my cheek with the back of his hand. 'I'll miss you.'

The house would feel so empty once he had left and my throat thickening, I told him so.

'But your house is full of cats,' he teased.

I spluttered a laugh. 'But there are times when it's nice to be the one held rather than the one holding.'

His fingertips ran down my neck. 'I'll be holding you again,' he promised, 'as soon as I can.'

He kissed me one last time and then he let me go, and tears blurred my eyes as I watched him drive away, certain he must have taken part of me with him.

It wasn't until Tuesday that Lou sussed out the reason for the change in my demeanour and instantly she dialled my shop where I was sitting upstairs in a dreamy haze, staring out of the window but seeing nothing except the perfect weekend which had flown so quickly by. I had fallen in love before but forgotten that it could be as painful as it was exciting and since Dan had gone home, all I could think about was how soon I could follow him there.

'I've heard you're dating a hottie,' Lou said. 'Why am I always the last to know?'

'Where did you hear that?' I asked her, frowning. Now she knew my secret there was no stopping it from spreading and I wondered who was responsible.

'From mum,' she replied, 'who heard it from Izzie, Sian's mum, and Sian saw it for herself so don't tell me it's all lies.'

'Well done Sherlock. Am I doing anything else I should know about?'

'Why do you think I'm calling?' Lou replied, as though that was obvious.

I wandered over to my desk and leant against it. 'Did Sian also say she was with Sophie at the time?'

Lou was speechless for an instant and then repeated, 'Sophie? As in *the* Sophie?

'Yep,' I confirmed.

'No!' Lou exclaimed. 'Did you speak to her? Are you okay?'

'No I didn't and yes I am, now at least.'

'I swear if I ever saw her again-' Lou began but I interrupted her.

'Lou, I don't really want to talk about that. I played out the same scenario in my head many times but when it actually happened...'

'What?' Lou prompted.

'I dunno. I didn't come out with the long powerful speech about how I'd thought she was my best friend but she'd betrayed me, like in the movies. In fact I couldn't say anything. I just...felt dreadful.' I sighed and put my head in my hand. 'For a second I felt right back at square one again.'

'But then you remembered you were having dinner with a hot guy,' Lou put in.

I huffed a small laugh. 'Yeah, well that helped.'

'So who is he?' she cried impatiently. 'Spill the beans!'

I realised I was grinning and it didn't fade as I told her about Dan, how we'd met, and that he'd just spent the weekend here.

'Wow!' was all she kept saying. 'Why didn't you say something before? You're so lucky. I can't believe you just bumped into him in the middle of nowhere.'

'And all thanks to a cat,' I added.

'Oh that reminds me,' Lou said excitably. 'Check your emails. I've sent you something.'

Frowning I turned to the laptop and got up my emails. 'What's this?' I asked, clinking on a link in a message from her.

'It's so cute, you're going to love it,' she promised.

It took me to a video on YouTube of a kitten which was squeaking in his sleep, his whiskers and ears twitching.

'Is it working?' Lou asked.

'Yeah,' I said, smiling.

'Great, huh?' she said. 'There are loads of videos like this. Some are so funny. I don't suppose your cats do anything special do they?'

'Am I still talking to Lou?' I teased. 'Louise Hunt?'

'What?' she appealed.

'I'm just surprised you like this stuff. You're hardly a cat lover.'

'I am. Well...kind of. Who doesn't like them? People at work send me these videos all the time. These cats are famous. There's another one where this cat plays granny's footsteps with the camera, just like we did as kids, you remember? Can Modi do that?'

'No,' I laughed.

'Maybe you should train him. He could be famous.'

'I'm not sure he could handle fame,' I jested. 'He's a bit shy.'

'So when do I get to meet him?'

'Modi?' I frowned.

'No, Dan.'

'Slow down Lou. I barely get to see enough of him myself.'

'When are you going there next?'

'I don't know yet. I'm going to have to ask Charlie to cover for me for another weekend.'

'You'll bring him to mum's surprise birthday bash won't you?'

'That's still going ahead then?' I said.

'Oh yeah! It's going to be great.'

'Then I'll bring him along,' I promised, but I didn't know when I made it that it was a promise I wouldn't be able to keep.

THIRTEEN

I took a deep breath and knocked on my parent's front door. It was a moment I had been dreading all week because I knew that once over the threshold I was destined to spend an entire evening in Karen's company. Ryan had called a couple of days ago to say he was taking a short trip up north and that on the way back he was stopping in at Mum and Dad's.

'It'll be fine,' Dan had assured me on the phone once I'd relayed my predicament.

'I just wish I was there with you instead,' I'd told him, nibbling my thumb nail, but Charlie had asked for the weekend off.

'I know, me too, but it can't be helped. You never know, you might even enjoy yourself tonight,' he'd dare suggest.

I'd laughed at that. 'I doubt it, not with her there.'

I knocked on my parent's door again and straightened out my dress as though checking there were no chinks in my armour.

'Hello Harriet,' my mum said as she opened the door.

The house smelt of Yorkshire Puddings and for an instant I was whisked back to my childhood. Not much had changed in the small cottage I had called home until my early twenties and as I rubbed the soles of my ballet pumps on the doormat, I glanced up the staircase and glimpsed my old bedroom door at the top.

'How are you? Everything all right?' I asked as I followed my mum to the kitchen.

'Oh yes, great,' she said. She was in a good mood which surprised me considering she usually got stressed when cooking for guests but then when I reached the kitchen I discovered she had a helping hand.

'Hattie, how are you?' Karen beamed. She was leaning over the hob and having seasoned whatever was simmering in the pan, she replaced the lid and walked over.

'Fine thank you,' I smiled politely and we stepped into an awkward embrace. 'You?' I asked as she let me go.

'Fabulous,' she replied, her thin lips still stretched wide.

'I brought some wine,' I said to my mum.

'Just put it on the side,' she told me.

I could feel Karen's gaze watching my every move, and she raised her severely plucked eyebrows as she considered my outfit. Her oval face was framed with mousey brown hair, she was a little overweight but proud of the cleavage which came with it and as always, it was aptly on show.

'How are the cats?' she asked.

I cleared my throat, not keen to broach the subject. 'They're well.'

'How many do you have again?' she asked, feigning uncertainty.

'Five,' my mum replied for me as she pushed a basket of sliced French bread into my hand. 'Will you take this through on your way Harriet,' she said. 'They're in the living room.'

I was only too happy to oblige.

'Hello Hattie,' my dad smiled, pushing back his chair and climbing to his feet so he could squeeze me in a hug.

'Hey Harriet,' Ryan grinned, standing too.

'Hi, how was the trip?' I asked as I stepped into his open arms. By the age of sixteen my brother had grown taller than our dad and unlike back then he now kept his curly hair cut short. He had always loved sport and kept in shape and since moving south his accent had taken on a different twang to my own.

'It was good, yeah,' he said. 'I went for work primarily but decided to make a small holiday of it.'

'Tell her about the house,' my dad chipped in. 'Rosé, Hattie?' my dad asked as he went to pour me a glass.

'Please,' I said and I sat down.

'Well I'm doing some drawings for this Palladian mansion,' Ryan told me. 'It's fantastic. Early eighteenth century.'

'Sounds impressive,' I said, intrigued.

'It is, very. Unfortunately one wing though is in a bad way, which is why I'm involved.'

That was when the door opened and Karen walked in with a plate of Yorkshire Puddings.

'If you ask me it's a white elephant,' she stated as she put them down on the table. 'The whole thing needs so much work.'

She didn't seem to recognise that no one was asking

her but she surged on.

'Maybe after a lot of modernisation it could be made into something useful, a hotel perhaps, but imagine how much that would cost.' She sat down and looked at Ryan. 'It's like all these houses you keep showing me. They need too much work. I want to buy somewhere I can move straight into, not a crumbling ruin.'

I caught Ryan sigh but Karen's gaze had already moved on and she reached for the wine.

'How is the house hunt going?' my dad asked.

'We can't seem to agree,' Ryan said, 'as you just heard. I found this beautiful little place but Karen insisted the kitchen wasn't big enough.'

'It was tiny,' she cried, raising her wine glass to her lips. 'I've seen bigger wardrobes. You know I like a good sized kitchen Ry.'

'I hope you're all hungry!' my mum said as she walked into the room.

'That smells good,' my dad smiled and we all watched as my mum placed a large casserole in the middle of the table.

'I'll put it out Linda,' Karen smiled and she reached for the ladle and the first of five plates, exercising a precision of presentation with each.

'It's lovely,' my dad said, smiling across at my mum.

'Thank Karen,' she said, instantly passing off the praise and looking over at her daughter-in-law with a grin. 'How is work by the way Karen?' she asked.

I reached for the basket of bread and picked up a piece, then tore it in two as Karen began a ten minute monologue. She was head chef at a chic restaurant and she loved to tell anyone who would listen how she had doggedly climbed the ladder to the top. The reviews were all exceedingly complimentary and lecturing us on the hierarchy of her kitchen, she spoke of the rest of the staff as though they were soldiers carrying out her orders with undying loyalty.

'Don't you find it hard sometimes,' my mum asked, 'working in such a male dominated environment?'

Karen laughed a cruel laugh and then said, 'I may be a woman but they know who's in charge.'

'I should imagine it's quite a stressful job,' I said, deciding I better join in with the conversation. 'All those tempers flaring.'

She fixed me with her cold grey eyes. 'I never lose my temper,' she replied and then she took another gulp of wine.

I didn't believe her for an instant.

'Dad was telling me you've been up north yourself Harriet,' Ryan said.

'Yes,' I smiled. 'To the Lake District, just for a short holiday, not business.'

At that point both my mum and dad stopped eating and looked at me, as though waiting for me to embellish and tell them something myself about the stranger I was rumoured to be dating. I took a deep breath and decided to.

'Actually I met someone there.'

Now Ryan and Karen stopped eating too and out of the corner of my eye I saw my mum nudge my dad's arm as though to say *here we go*.

'His name's Dan.'

'That's great Hattie,' Ryan smiled warmly.

'What does he do?' Karen asked.

'He's a postman,' I told them, 'and a talented photographer.'

'And does he know that you've got loads of cats?' she giggled.

My gaze fell as I chewed over those words. 'Yes, he knows I have five cats,' I said evenly.

'You know,' she continued, still giggling, 'I can imagine you as an old woman in your little cottage surrounded by hundreds of cats. A bit of a crazy cat lady.'

'Oh really,' I said. I wasn't sure how I was supposed to take that as anything other than an insult and judging from everyone else's expressions they were wondering the same.

Ryan cleared his throat. 'I don't know why you're picking on Harriet, Karen. That friend of yours has got just as many cats.'

'Not *as* many,' Karen retorted.

'Almost,' Ryan insisted.

'Yes well it's different with Ellie. She's not...'

Karen stopped herself before saying divorced but we all knew the word that she had juggled on the end of her tongue.

'I think you've probably had a bit too much wine Karen,' Ryan said, breaking the silence that she had singlehandedly crafted.

'Don't be silly Ry, it's Saturday night and Hattie knows I'm only joking, don't you Hattie?'

'Sure,' I nodded but I was lying as much as she was.

We finished eating the main course using words in a minimalistic fashion and the spaces were filled with an increase in alcohol consumption.

'Let me help you Linda,' Karen insisted as my mum began to clear away the dirty dishes. 'Did I see that you made your famous apple crumble for dessert?'

'Yes, I put in some cinnamon this time, like you suggested.'

Once Karen had followed my mum from the room,

chattering non-stop as though the more she talked the sooner we might forget what she'd said before, Ryan looked at me and said, 'Just ignore her.'

I grinned but it was only skin deep. Karen had hit her target and it hurt.

'I'll be back in a minute,' I said, and I left the table and headed for the bathroom.

The eyes which stared back at me in the mirror over the sink looked ready to leak and I screwed them shut. *Don't listen to her, don't let her make you feel like this*, I told myself sternly. I splashed some cool water on my face, breathed deeply and then headed back into the fray.

By the time the crumble was dished out, the tempo of the evening had returned and although Karen kept talking, she was happy with just my mum as an audience. As they enthusiastically discussed a fat-free victoria sponge recipe, my dad asked me more about Dan, an interrogation at heart but disguised, not particularly successfully, by an air of genuine curiosity.

'You don't have to worry dad, honestly,' I assured him. 'I'm not about to fall in love with another Richard. He couldn't be more different.'

'And he's a photographer you say?' he asked.

'Yes, a very good one.'

'You were always quite creative yourself,' he said. 'I think it's a shame you stopped drawing.'

'I've actually started again,' I told him. 'Just recently.'

'Wow, he must be a good influence,' he smiled. 'I suppose you'll be heading back up there as soon as you can?'

'Yeah,' I admitted, trying not to blush like a love-struck teenager.

'By the way did you hear Will's finished with Mel?' Ryan said.

Neither of us had.

'That didn't last long,' my dad said.

'Do they ever?' Ryan replied with a grin my dad and I both mimicked.

'I don't know how he does it,' I sighed, 'breaking all those hearts.'

'I think they know beforehand it's only a short term contract where Will's involved,' Ryan said and I supposed he was right.

'Have you heard from Ollie at all?' I asked them.

'Err, yeah,' my dad said. 'Ollie rang the other day didn't he Linda?'

'Ollie?' my mum said in a tone that suggested my dad was very wrong. 'No, not since the other weekend.'

I frowned.

'Why? What's up?' my dad asked.

'I just can't get hold of him recently,' I replied.

'He's busy, that's all,' Ryan assured me.

'I know,' I nodded though I was still niggled with doubt.

Dad nudged Ryan on the arm. 'Have you heard his new song?'

'Yeah, it's catchy!' my brother smiled.

Karen laughed. 'Catchy like a bramble!'

We all stopped and looked at her, a silence settling across the table for a second time, and I wondered how she was going to talk her way out of this one.

FOURTEEN

I sat on the windowsill in my studio, looking back across the busy room but not seeing anything of it. Anything except my reflection in an old mirror leaning against the opposite wall and Karen's vision of me. She had said it more bluntly than anyone else had yet dared; that it wasn't normal to have five cats. People often teased and I shrugged off their comments but I couldn't deny that deep inside I was beginning to fear they may be right. Modi and his sisters had come out of nowhere at the loneliest, most difficult point of my life and helped me through it. Without them I don't know if I'd have made it in one piece and in return I had invested a lot of love in them. Should I be ashamed of that, I wondered. Did that mean I was a crazy cat lady? If so, then so be it I found myself thinking with a sudden spurt of determination. I sighed and leant my head back against the glass. But how long would it be until Dan realised he didn't want to be with one?

'Harriet?'

I looked to the top of the staircase as Charlie called me and a few seconds later she appeared, holding the phone and grinning, her cheeks bright red.

'Call for you,' she said.

'Who is it?' I asked, curiosity peeling me from the window sill.

'Your brother, Ollie.'

I smiled, her flushed expression suddenly making sense, and then took the phone. 'Thanks Charlie.'

'Hey Hattie, sorry I didn't get back to you sooner,' was the first thing Ollie said.

I felt relieved to hear his voice but didn't tell him that he'd been getting me worried. 'That's okay, is everything all right?'

'Err...yeah,' he said, his answer not full of his usual confidence and my fingers tightened around the phone.

'You sure? It doesn't sound it,' I told him.

There was a pause and then he said, 'Hattie, can I come stay? Just for a short while?'

'Sure,' I said. 'That's always okay.'

'Thanks.'

'Should I be worried about you Ollie?'

'No, no, I just need a bit of a break,' he said.

'Well it'll be good to see you. I'll pick you up from the train station okay? When are you coming?'

'Wednesday all right?

'Yeah,' I nodded. 'Wednesday's fine.'

When Wednesday morning came I dug out some clean sheets for the spare room but didn't get as far as making the bed after almost tripping over Mona halfway up the staircase. She was sitting huddled, her head bowed, and I frowned and crouched down.

'You okay darling?' I asked her, reaching out to

stroke her head. Her reaction was sluggish and hearing the crunch of cats eating, I looked back over my shoulder and could just see the others still eating their breakfast in the kitchen. 'You're not hungry?'

That couldn't be good, I thought to myself. Mona was always hungry. My eyes wandered up the staircase and when I spotted sick a couple of treads up my heart began to pound with worry. Suddenly panic whisked up my thoughts like a hurricane and then scattered them haphazardly. I didn't know what to do, I realised as I looked back at Mona, her eyes heavy and coat dull. I had never had an ill cat before. Could it be serious, I thought, going through every possibility no matter how irrational and then abruptly I turned around, headed back downstairs, and snatched up the phone.

'So is everything okay?' Charlie asked as I finally made it to the shop gone eleven o'clock.

'Yeah,' I nodded, setting the cat carrier down on the counter, and Charlie peered through the bars.

'You poor little thing,' she said softly as Mona sleepily looked back at her.

'The vet thinks she just ate something that disagreed with her.'

'We all have our rough days huh?' Charlie said.

'She scared me a bit,' I admitted.

'I could tell from your voice when you rang,' she grinned.

I looked across at her with a small smile of my own. 'You think I'm a worry wart.'

Charlie laughed. 'No I don't.'

'It's okay,' I shrugged. 'I know I am. I'm as bad as a new mother. Speaking of which,' I added as Charlie's hand fell to her stomach, 'have you thought of any names yet?'

'I like Charlotte if it's a girl,' she said shyly. 'Jack if it's a boy.'

'Sweet,' I nodded, smiling. 'I like them.'

'Greg suggested Kieran. I know,' she laughed when she saw my grimace. 'No way.'

'You must be getting excited?' I asked.

She nodded. 'A bit nervous too actually.' She looked back at Mona. 'I've never even had a cat.'

'You'll do fine,' I assured her. 'I know you will.'

Mona spent the day with me in my office, sitting in a pool of sunshine that trickled through the window. Towards the end of the afternoon she even ventured from her bed, her nose sniffing the air, and I smiled, certain that meant she must be on the mend.

'Your appetite's back then?' I said as she hovered by my feet whilst I opened a packet of digestives, her ears twitching to the rustle of the wrapper.

'Who's in the back?' Ollie asked when I picked him up on the way home.

'That's Mona,' I replied.

'I'm guessing it wasn't take your pet to work day.'

I smiled. 'No, she had to visit the vet but everything's okay now. What about you?' I looked across at him, sitting in the passenger seat as he heaved a sigh.

'Glad to have a break. Tensions have been getting a bit high.'

'Between the band?' I asked.

He nodded. 'It's got to the point where Johnny and Simon can barely stand to be in the same room together and you know how Andy was always better mates with Simon, so I'm the one left hanging in the middle trying to keep everything together.'

When we got home I made two large mugs of tea and he dropped onto the sofa.

'What are they fighting about?' I asked as he wrapped his hands around the mug.

'We work in close proximity every day,' he began. 'Sometimes it's great fun but other times it's not so easy. The more we get recognised the bigger the egos get, one accuses the other of not pulling their weight, and before you know it there's a wedge driven between them and it just grows and grows. They don't like playing together anymore,' he admitted. 'They seem to have forgotten that we started this for the music. I can tell that their hearts aren't really in it, the way they should be. The way it used to be. I'm just dreading the day when one or the other decides they've had enough and leaves. I've worked so hard to get here and I'm worried they're just going to chuck it away.' He ran a hand through his hair, his face grey with exasperation.

'You've tried talking to them?'

'Not together. And Simon's particularly stubborn.'

I remembered them all well. They'd been best mates since the beginning of high school. Simon was the front man, Johnny the guitarist and Andy played bass.

'You guys go a long way back,' I told him. 'And I know they listen to you. If you want to hold it together then you've got to remind them of that hunger you all shared to make music. Forget the fame for five minutes and take them back to their roots. You were the one who started this band Ollie. You were the one who got the first gig back in that dingy bar. You can pull them through the tough times too, I know it.'

'I hope you're right,' he said.

'You know I'm right Ollie. Like you said, you've

worked so hard to get here, you're not going to let it slip away.'

He took a sip of his tea and sank a little deeper into the cushions.

'But for now I'm going to cook us something to eat little brother,' I told him, 'and you can relax.'

He smiled for the first time. 'That sounds good. I'm sick of takeaways.'

I made lasagne, Ollie's favourite, and while it was in the oven Dan rang. My elbows on the worktop I told him about my day and from where I stood I could see Modi tiptoeing across the sofa towards Ollie's lap who was strumming absent-mindedly on his acoustic guitar.

'I heard on the great-vine that you're seeing someone,' Ollie said as we ate later at the kitchen table.

I smiled self-consciously. 'Yeah, his name's Dan.'

'And he's from the north.'

'News travels fast in this family huh?' I laughed.

'I think it's great,' he grinned. 'I'm happy for you.'

'Thanks,' I blushed.

'How long have you been together?'

'About four weeks I think.'

'And it' not too difficult going back and forth to see each other?'

'Well it's not easy...' I admitted, 'but he's worth it.'

'Were you going up there this weekend?'

I shook my head. 'No, you're here.'

'But if I wasn't?'

'That's irrelevant Ollie because you are here and you're welcome to stay as long as you want.'

'So you cancelled on him? Just?'

I laughed. 'Honestly? Then yes, I cancelled.'

'Why?'

'You asked to stay over the weekend so-'

'Hattie I want you to go,' he interrupted. 'Don't stick around for me. Have fun and I'll house-sit for you.'

I frowned and sipped my wine.

'I'm serious,' he insisted.

'You don't mind if I just go and leave you to babysit my house and five cats?'

'Not at all,' he smiled. 'We get on and you'll need someone to feed them while you're away anyway.'

'You're not going to have a house party are you?' I teased.

He pulled a face. 'That's the last thing I want right now.'

A smile crept across my face as I imagined heading back up to the lakes.

'Call him back,' Ollie told me. 'Tell him you're coming after all.'

So I did and as soon as the call ended, the phone rang again.

'Hello,' I said, putting it to my ear.

'Hi.'

It was Richard again and my gaze shot through to the living room where Ollie was watching television, as though afraid he might have heard my ex-husband's voice from there.

'I didn't expect you to call again,' I said flatly.

He hesitated then said, 'I was wondering how you were.'

'Really?'

'I didn't mean to upset you last time I called Hattie.'

'Oh you couldn't upset me anymore than you already have Richard. Now do you really care about how I feel or is this just about your guitar again?'

He took a second to consider his answer then said, 'Can I come over?'

157

I laughed. 'I've told you it's not here.'

'Can I check?'

I sighed. 'If you really want to but I won't be here. I'm going away. Ollie will be house sitting. I can let him know you're coming.'

'Ollie?'

'My brother, yeah.'

'Ah, it doesn't matter then.'

'No?' I asked, feigning surprise although it was the response I'd expected. 'Well you wouldn't have found it anyway,' I told him.

'When will you be back?'

'Richard seriously, I don't have anything of yours. Whatever you left I threw out months ago but it didn't include your guitar. You didn't even play it for years when it *was* hanging around. What's up? Have you decided to give it another shot?'

'Something like that,' he mumbled.

I sighed and let a silence take over.

'You can't keep calling me Richard,' I eventually said. 'Let me move on. It's not been easy these last few months and you're not helping.'

He was quiet for a moment. 'Okay, I understand,' he said. 'I'm sorry. Goodbye then.'

'Bye Richard.'

I put down the phone and wandered back across the kitchen to where Mona was curled up asleep in a basket by the window. Placing my hand on her head as she flinched and squeaked in her sleep, it helped soothe her troubled dreams, but my fear would not fade so easily; my fear that Richard already knew his guitar wasn't here.

FIFTEEN

'Okay, the fridge, freezer and food cupboards are full so help yourself,' I told Ollie Friday morning. 'The water heater comes on every morning and night so you shouldn't have any problems with the shower, that being said the handle is a little lose on the bath so just be careful; I haven't got round to calling the plumber yet. Cat food is kept in the pantry, if they moan for anything special there's some milk for them in the fridge. I'm not expecting any calls but if there are any just take a number and tell them I'll get back to them next week. If you have time could you water the new seedlings outside each evening; I don't think any rain's expected. Um...' I frowned, trying to recall if there was anything else I'd forgotten.

Ollie stood across from me with Modi in his arms and a smile on his face. 'It's all right Harriet, I think I've got everything. We'll manage while you're away.'

I always felt anxious when going away for more than one night. There seemed so much to do and I'd spent all morning rushing around trying to make sure everything was organised but at last a smile lightened my concerned expression.

'Okay,' I nodded in concession. 'Thanks again for doing this.'

'No problem,' Ollie replied. 'Off you go, enjoy yourself.'

'You too,' I told him, 'and you Modi,' I smiled, running a gentle finger between his ears as he looked back at me as though wondering where I was rushing off to. 'I'll see you soon.'

Suddenly he decided he wanted to wriggle free from Ollie's arms and climb into mine.

'I'm sorry little guy,' I said, putting him down. 'I've got to go.'

He watched me pick up my bag and then followed me to the door.

'See you Sunday,' Ollie called as I climbed into my car.

'Yeah, see you Sunday,' I smiled but the smile fell as I put the car into gear and then Modi began trotting towards me down the garden path, the small ginger cat slowly disappearing in my rear view mirror as I drove away.

I knocked on Dan's front door and took a deep breath as I smoothed the creases out of my dress.

'Oh hello,' I said, taken by surprise when it slowly creaked open and a metre tall Spiderman in little blue Wellingtons peered at me through the gap, his fingers clinging to the brass door handle.

'Hello,' came a small reply, his voice muffled behind his mask.

I assumed the boy standing on the doormat was Joe

and I had not expected to meet him today.

'Is your dad at home?' I asked.

Slowly he began to nod and then span around as we both heard footsteps approach us.

'Harriet,' Dan said when he appeared, his smile broad as he pulled the door open wider and placed a hand on his son's shoulder. 'Joe, this is my friend Harriet, the one I was telling you about. Harriet, this is my son Joe.'

At that Joe pulled up his mask and for the first time I saw his face, ruddy cheeked and dark haired which he shook from his eyes as he looked up at Dan.

'Dad! I'm Spiderman,' he frowned, his nose puckering.

I smiled at the little boy's indignation and crouching to his level, decided to play along. 'Hello Spiderman. I like your outfit.'

Joe smiled bashfully, revealing pink gums where his two bottom front teeth had recently fallen out.

'Let's let Harriet in then fella,' Dan said. 'You can let her try one of those cookies you made earlier with a drink, yeah?'

'Can I have one too?' he asked, his eyes wide.

'Of course,' Dan grinned and once he had ushered his son back into the house, he took my bag.

'I missed you,' he whispered, leaning close to kiss me.

'I missed you too,' I replied, breathing in his scent.

'I hope you don't mind Joe being here. After you said you couldn't come I volunteered to take him for the weekend and then you changed your mind-'

'It's fine,' I interrupted, kissing him softly again. 'Honestly. I'm glad I get to meet him. He's adorable.'

Dan chuckled. 'He's quite a little chatterbox too... as

you'll soon find out.'

He closed the door and we followed Joe into the kitchen who had already clambered onto a chair at the kitchen table and was hovering over a plate of freshly baked cookies. By the looks of it he was trying to decide which was the biggest.

'Um, it smells good in here,' I said.

'Tea?' Dan asked, squeezing my hand as he brushed past on his way to the kettle.

'Please,' I smiled.

'You want a hot chocolate Joe?'

Joe nodded enthusiastically and then returned to the cookie debate.

'I'd have that one on top if I were you,' I said, sitting down at the table too.

He looked up at me, confused why as it was clearly not the largest.

'It's not as big,' I admitted, 'but it's got more chocolate chips.'

His brow furrowed as he considered this for a moment and then abruptly he whisked it up, beaming with satisfaction that he'd made a good choice as he held it in both hands.

'Have you offered Harriet a cookie Joe?'

Joe looked at his dad and then me, his eyes belying the fact that he was still a little unsure of the stranger in his kitchen. 'Would you like one?' he asked in a small voice as he pushed the plate slightly in my direction.

'Thank you,' I smiled and I picked one up. 'Um, it's delicious,' I told him as I took a bite.

'Cookies are Joe's speciality, aren't they mate?' Dan said, returning to us and choosing one himself.

Joe nodded. 'I'm good at making cake's too,' he said.

'Wow, what a useful little chef,' I grinned.

'I got a cooking set for my birthday,' he said. 'Do you want to see?'

'Okay,' I nodded.

Joe dashed off to the kitchen cupboards and retrieved a hessian bag with a drawing of a cupcake on the side. He brought it back to the table and climbed onto his chair and then tipped the bag up so that all the contents spilled out.

'Take it easy fella,' Dan said as he caught a star shaped cookie cutter before it rolled off the side of the table. He returned it to the assorted pile of brightly coloured objects amongst which were silicon cake cases, spatulas, a little recipe book, and a rolling pin.

'I've got an apron too,' he told me, his words flowing more confidently as he showed me the components of his baking set.

'Yeah?'

'But it's in the wash,' Dan reminded him. 'There was a mishap with some golden syrup and a bag of flour earlier,' he added, looking at me.

'Sounds messy,' I replied.

Joe giggled and nodded. 'Dad got angry.'

I bit my lip as Dan looked a little embarrassed that that part of the story had been leaked. 'It wasn't that I was angry Joe,' he insisted. 'It's just I was trying to keep the place tidy.'

'Because your friend was coming,' Joe finished and Dan looked across at me even more embarrassed than before.

I held his gaze as my lips stretched into a grin.

'I'm going to make the drinks,' Dan said decisively before he let himself grin too, and he got to his feet and headed back to the kettle even though it was yet to boil.

'Remember to use my special mug,' Joe called after

him.

'I always do,' Dan said over his shoulder.

Joe finished his cookie, the table top aptly showered in crumbs, and then said thoughtfully, 'There's a girl in my class at school called Harriet.'

'Is there? Are you friends?' I asked.

He shook his head, his expression a little shocked by the mere prospect of the idea. 'No, she's a girl. I don't like girls.'

'Oh dear,' I said, thinking aloud as I wondered where this put me.

'You might change your mind about that when you're older,' Dan chuckled.

Joe frowned seriously. 'No I won't.'

'Who's your friend then?' I asked him.

'Ryan, and Tom too.'

'I have a brother called Ryan.'

Joe thought about this for a moment and then said, 'I don't have a brother. But I have a little sister. Her name's Chloe.'

I was taken aback for a moment and looked at Dan to find that he was already looking at me. He speedily walked over with the hot drinks and sat down next to me with an expression that suggested he wished he had spoken of this privately beforehand.

'Joe's mum has just had a baby,' he said, 'with her husband Rick.'

I released the breath I'd held whilst waiting for an explanation and, looking at Dan and his fearful expression as he tried to read mine, I felt a pang of sympathy for him. I knew how it felt to be replaced. I reached for his hand underneath the table and gave it a little squeeze.

'She cries all the time,' Joe complained.

Dan passed his son his drink and the little boy blew the surface fiercely, creating waves of hot chocolate.

'Yes you can have another,' Dan told him as he looked at the plate of cookies. 'Harriet? Do you want one?'

'I won't say no,' I smiled.

For several minutes Joe was quiet as he cautiously sipped his drink but his gaze darted back and forth between Dan and I as we spoke of events since we had last seen one another. He'd sold a couple of photos to someone who had seen his work in the café.

'It's not much but...'

'It's still a sale,' I finished for him. 'That's great.'

He was thinking of setting up a website for his work and I told him that was a good idea.

'You should definitely do that,' I encouraged.

'Actually I err... I have something for you,' Dan said.

'You do?' I said, surprised.

'Yeah, a present. I'll be back in a moment.'

Dan left the kitchen and Joe, suddenly looking very alert, asked, 'Is it your birthday?'

I shook my head. 'No,' I replied, smiling.

'Here,' Dan said as he returned and placed a large rectangular present in my hands.

My smile grew wider as I looked at him.

'Open it!' Joe cried excitedly, so I did, and once I'd peeled away the paper I held a wooden frame in both hands, contained in which was a photograph of myself holding Modi.

'It's the photo you took just before you left, isn't it?' I asked.

Dan nodded.

I had photos of my cats but, living alone, no one had ever been there before to take one of me with them.

'It's wonderful,' I said softly as I admired my gift. He'd captured the moment perfectly; I who usually shied away from photos of myself, caught in the snare of my own gaze which seemed so at ease and full of love for the little cat whose head was resting on my shoulder. 'Thank you so much,' I said, looking at Dan. 'I love it, I really do.'

Dan's smile grew to match my own.

'What is it? Let me see!' Joe cried.

I turned it to show him and watched as his eyes wandered around the frame.

'Who's that?' he frowned.

'That's my cat,' I told him.

'He's funny,' Joe giggled. 'I like cats. My granny's got one. His name's Teddy because he looks like a teddy bear.'

Joe's little giggle was infectious and I started laughing too.

'I've got a hamster. Do you want to see him?'

'Okay,' I said and Joe pushed himself off his chair and skipped across to Indiana's cage. As Joe's back was turned I looked at Dan and mouthed, *I love you*.

'I love you too,' he said quietly.

'This is Indiana,' Joe said as he returned to the table and stopped beside my chair. He was holding the hamster against his chest with both hands as tenderly as a mother with a new born, and there was a gentle smile on his face as he looked down at the little creature.

'He's very cute,' I said.

'You can hold him if you want,' he said, 'but you have to be really careful,' he added seriously.

Dan laughed. 'Harriet won't hurt him fella.'

'I'll be careful,' I assured Joe, seeing the concern on his face. 'You can trust me.'

He passed Indiana over and I smiled as he scuttled about in my hands, his small feet tickling my skin.

'He likes you,' Joe smiled.

'That means Joe likes you,' Dan interpreted when his son had wandered from the room. Tired of grown-up talk he'd gone into the living room along with Indiana in his plastic ball, to play.

I heaved a sigh of relief. 'I passed the test huh?'

Dan smiled and then pulled me close.

'He's a sweet kid,' I said.

Dan nodded. 'Yeah, he's a good lad.'

His hands fell to my waist and we began moving in slow circles as though dancing except that there was no music for our steps to follow.

'Have you sold that gramophone we found?' Dan asked. 'I bet it went straight away didn't it?'

'Actually it hasn't made it quite as far as the shop yet,' I replied.

'What do you mean?'

For a moment I toyed with not telling the truth but then did. 'I can't bring myself to sell it,' I admitted. 'Not when every time I look at it I think of you.'

He smiled and I knew my cheeks were burning red.

'Have you tried the other vinyls?' he asked.

I nodded. 'But none are as good as that first one.'

'Hey, you never let me know how it went with your sister-in-law, Karen is it, last weekend.'

'Oh,' I said, a frown briefly taking hold of my features.

'That bad?' he asked.

'Just the usual,' I replied, but then shaking my head added, 'I'd rather not talk about it to be honest.'

For a moment he looked at me with an expression that asked *why not?*

'She doesn't deserve to be talked about. She brasses me off when she's around and when she's not I'd prefer not to think about her, no matter how much I would enjoy listing her fine qualities,' I jested.

'Then would you like some wine?' Dan asked as our dance took us over to the kitchen counter where a bottle of sweet white sat waiting.

I nodded. 'What's cooking?' The interior of the oven glowed and something was sizzling beneath a sheet of silver foil.

'Roast chicken,' Dan replied as he reached for two glasses.

'Need any help?' I asked.

'I thought you might say that.'

'Me, me, me!' Joe cried when Dan asked who wanted to pull the wish bone.

'Harriet?'

'No, it's okay, you boys go ahead,' I said, smiling as Joe hugged one side of the bone with his little finger and Dan the other.

'Okay, on three,' Dan told him, 'one, two, three.'

'Yay, I win!' Joe cried as the bone snapped and he came away with the larger half.

'Make a wish then,' Dan said.

Joe's face suddenly became serious and he stared at me across the table.

'Done it,' he said with a little nod several moments later and he dropped the bone onto his empty plate. 'What's for pudding dad?'

Dan made a small laugh. 'Give us a moment mate, we've only just finished.'

The table was still an array of dirty dishes and empty glasses.

'But what *will* be for pudding?' he asked impatiently.

Dan glanced across at me with a grin that said, *see, he's not always easy*. 'Well Harriet brought an apple pie for us all,' he told his son.

Joe's eyes widened and he smiled excitedly. 'Can we have it with custard?'

'If you like,' Dan replied.

Joe nodded keenly and then looked at me and said, 'Thank you.'

'My pleasure,' I smiled.

Then Joe's little nose wrinkled as he thought of a question. 'How long are you going to stay?'

'Err...' I stumbled, as I heard Dan make a similarly embarrassed sound. I looked across at him and found he was wearing an apologetic expression.

'Harriet's going to stay with us for the weekend Joe.'

'The whole weekend?' he asked, looking a little awe-struck.

'Yeah,' Dan nodded.

Joe's smile reappeared. 'So she can come sailing with us tomorrow?'

'Of course,' Dan said. 'If you want to go sailing that is?' Dan asked me.

'I'd love to,' I told them, pleased that Joe looked genuinely excited at the prospect of someone new coming along.

'My dad's got a boat,' Joe said, looking at me again. 'It's an old one and he's fixing it. Sometimes I'm allowed to steer.'

I was reminded of the time that I had taken the wheel on the waters of Windermere Lake myself, back when Dan and I had barely known one another. Dan caught my eye and I knew he was thinking of that too.

'Dad says I have to wear a life jacket but I *can* swim.

I've got my red badge,' Joe said proudly.

'Wow, well done,' I smiled.

He took a gulp of squash from his plastic beaker and then looked again at his dad. 'Can we have pudding *now*?'

Both Dan and I laughed.

'All right, you win,' he said. 'You fetch the bowls, I'll clear the table-'

'And I'll get the pie,' I finished.

'I haven't played on a PlayStation since I was about twelve,' I said in my defence when Joe celebrated beating me for the third time in a row on a racing car game. 'And I wasn't very good at it back then.'

My excuses went ignored as he continued to race around in small circles on the carpet, pulling his pyjama top over his head like a footballer rejoicing his hat trick.

'Don't worry, I'm no good at it either,' Dan said, walking in and sitting next to me on the sofa.

'You're probably still better than me,' I told him.

'No, my dad's rubbish,' Joe said, coming to a halt beside me.

'Hey, cheeky,' Dan said, mock frowning. He picked up the controller that Joe had abandoned on the carpet and said, 'Come on, I'll challenge you to a race. Then we'll see.'

'Okay,' I grinned.

Following Joe's tuition I chose a car, a sleek red one that he said was the best, whilst Dan picked out a bright yellow one, and then hovering excitedly by my side he squeezed in as many tips as he could in the time it took the game to load.

'Hey, why aren't you helping me?' Dan complained.

Joe looked at me with a small smile and I matched it.

'I'll try my best for you,' I assured him.

Unfortunately though my best wasn't quite good enough and by the time Joe realised he'd backed the wrong team, Dan was an easy lap ahead of me. His jittery excitement began to fade as I crashed for the umpteenth time and a small frown settled on his face as his dad soared over the finishing line and began to gloat.

'I'm sorry, I didn't mean it,' Dan apologised.

He leant across and planted a light kiss on my cheek but then froze when he realised he'd got caught up in the spontaneity of the moment. We both looked at Joe but the tension in my shoulders relaxed when we found that he had turned away and had his head and shoulders immersed in a toy box and hadn't seen a thing. He reappeared clutching another game in his hand.

'It's almost bedtime mate,' Dan warned him.

'Please please please!' he pleaded. 'Just five minutes?'

I wondered whether Dan's guilty conscience of keeping a secret from his son affected his decision. He glanced at the clock and then nodded. 'Alright, five minutes.'

Joe hissed in triumph and darted to put the game in and it was more like ten times the allocated number of minutes before the controller was at last prised from his fingers and he was tucked up into bed.

I smiled as Dan trundled wearily back down the staircase and then fell onto the sofa beside me. Somehow the tired dad look made him more attractive than ever. I snuggled into him as he put an arm around me then looked up when he made a small laugh.

'What is it?' I asked, smiling.

'It was just something Joe said,' he replied with a small shake of the head.

'What did he say?'

Dan reached for my hand. 'He said I'm more fun when you're here.'

I laughed. 'Is that right? Could it be because you're not the worst on the PlayStation anymore?'

He grinned and kissed the back of my hand. 'How did you guess?'

'Best of three?' I said, nodding at the controller. 'Or did you have something else in mind?' I added with a suggestive smile.

'There was something...' he began and this time he kissed my lips.

My body melted at his touch and my mind could think of nothing but his hands as they slid beneath my clothes, his fingertips firing sharp bolts of excitement wherever they touched my skin. He pulled off his shirt and the sense of urgency grew, his lips breaking from mine only to wander down my neck which is when I heard it; a door somewhere upstairs creaked open.

'What was that?' I said, my voice barely a whisper.

'Dad?' came a small voice.

Dan stopped and let out a small groan and I found myself giggling as he dropped like a lead weight on top of me.

'No, no, no,' he cursed, his face in my shoulder.

'Dad?' Joe called again and footsteps sounded on the floorboards above, heading for the top of the staircase.

Slowly Dan heaved himself up and threw his t-shirt back over his head.

'I'll be back in a couple of minutes,' he promised, sluggishly climbing to his feet, his expression pained. 'Don't go anywhere?'

I shook my head and smiled. 'I'm not going anywhere.'

'I'm sorry,' he said.

'Don't be,' I told him. 'It's okay. Go.'

He smiled and leant back to kiss me, then straightened up just before Joe appeared at the top of the stairs.

'I'm coming mate,' he called. 'I'm coming.'

Joe held a teddy bear in one hand and mumbled something about being scared of the dark as Dan made his way up. He scooped his son up into his arms and kissed him on the forehead.

'Did I forget to leave the door cracked open?'

From my spot on the sofa I heard Joe say *yes, he had* and then Dan's footsteps head back to Joe's room.

It had been a good afternoon. Joe was a great kid, as sweet as his dad, and the fact that Dan had chosen to introduce us meant a lot. And yet as fun as it had been, meeting his son had also been a little scary. Suddenly the prospect of one day becoming a step-mum was very real and I didn't know if I would be a good one, if good ones even existed I pondered as the well-known stereotypes from children's fairy tales blockaded all rational thought. Would Joe resent a third wheel butting into the close relationship he shared with his dad? Would it alter things between Dan and I? Worry began to niggle away at my insecurities, the questions growing in number and then escalating out of reason, but when Dan reappeared I hoped I was worrying needlessly because I knew, as his eyes met mine, that he was the one I wanted to spend the rest of my life with.

SIXTEEN

'Can you help me?' Joe asked.

He was struggling to fasten the buckle of his life jacket and putting down the basket I'd been carrying, I knelt down in front of him.

'Sure can,' I smiled and I clipped the clasps together. 'There, ready to climb aboard?'

He nodded enthusiastically and surprised me by reaching for my hand. Dan was already on deck of the boat and I passed over the picnic basket before Joe and I stepped aboard together.

'Everyone okay?' Dan asked, smiling as he noticed that Joe was still holding my hand. His young face displayed a mix of excitement and trepidation as Lake Windermere rocked us gently from side to side.

'Yeah we're okay,' I said, giving Joe's hand a small friendly squeeze. 'You want to sit down?' I asked him.

'Can I steer?' he said.

I looked to Dan to answer this one who said he could very soon, but he would start them off until they were away from the pier and all the other boats. So Joe and I sat down. His legs were too short to reach the deck and he swung his feet excitedly back and forth as we watched Dan untie the mooring ropes, and when he felt brave enough his hand wriggled out of mine.

It was a perfect day for it. The sun was warm on our faces and the wind gentle enough that the waves were not intimidating. The hills that climbed all around us were a beautiful emerald green and the blue sky betrayed not one whisper of cloud. Joe was jittery, eager to have his go, and kept talking at high speed, only pausing to take gulps of air.

'One day you'll wear out that tongue of yours,' Dan warned him, looking over at us, and once I'd reassured him that his dad was joking and it was impossible for his tongue to wear out, the worried look vanished from Joe's face and he began to giggle.

'Come on then, over you come,' Dan told him and Joe rushed to the wheel.

'Let go dad,' he frowned, trying to prise off Dan's hand that was waiting to make sure Joe had control.

'You're a bossy one today aren't you?' Dan laughed and he ruffled his son's hair which brought on another complaint from Joe.

Dan sat down next to me and we grinned at one another.

'Harriet, look at me! Harriet, look! Harriet?'

Joe had to call my name three times before I dragged my gaze away from Dan.

'Wow! Look at you,' I smiled. 'Captain Joe.'

We meandered across the lake until Joe's stomach told us it was time for lunch and despite wanting to skip anything savoury and delve straight into the cupcakes, we persuaded him to have a sandwich first.

'Look over there,' I told him, pointing towards a group of people on the shore who were waving at our small lone boat bobbing gently on the vast expanse of water. As we waved back it struck me that I was no longer the spectator on the side-line. My life had changed so much since that cup of tea with my parents when I'd told them that I felt as much. What I'd found on my subsequent trip to the Lake District hadn't exactly been what I'd expected and yet it had turned out to be everything I needed. I was something to someone again and Dan and Joe had filled that gap that Modi and his sisters had been keeping warm during the times I'd been convinced that the only love I would ever know again was the unconditional love of a pet.

I wondered if from the shore we looked like a perfect, happy family. It certainly felt that way. A contented smile settled on my face and I heard myself sigh.

'You okay?' Dan asked gently, mistaking it for a sigh of fatigue.

I nodded. 'Couldn't be happier,' I said quietly.

His eyes lingered for a moment on my lips but Joe had finished his yoghurt and presenting the empty carton to his dad, had his eyes on us.

'Thank you very much,' Dan frowned, trying to dodge the dirty spoon that Joe was still wielding wildly as he took the pot from him. 'You want some tea?' he asked me.

Inside the boat's cabin Dan had a small gas ring and all the essentials for a cuppa.

'Yeah, okay,' I smiled.

'Hot chocolate for you Joe?' he asked.

Joe nodded. 'And can I have my cake now?'

'You can have your cake now,' Dan smiled.

As Dan disappeared inside the cabin, Joe prised the lid off the cake tin and snatched up the one he'd had his eyes on since icing them that morning. Once he'd peeled off the paper wrapper he took a large bite out of it but before he took a second he stopped and looked at me.

'Harriet?' he said, lines appearing on his brow as though he was troubled by something.

'Joe?' I replied with a grin.

'Are you my dad's girlfriend?'

That wasn't the question I'd been expecting and my first reaction was a small nervous laugh.

'Err...' I stumbled, glancing to the cabin door and hoping Dan would reappear. Joe was still staring, wanting his answer, and I decided it was only fair to tell him the truth. I took a deep breath and nodded.

'I thought so,' he replied instantly, fidgeting in his seat.

I didn't need to ask him what he thought, he was grinning like the Cheshire Cat.

'What are you laughing at?' Dan asked Joe when he came back out on deck.

'You've got a girlfriend,' he said.

Dan's expression was a mix between a frown and a grin and he looked at me.

'I'm sorry,' I told him, grinning too. 'He beat it out of me.'

The frowning part of Dan's expression faded and he sat down. Joe meanwhile, his detective work complete, took another bit of his cake.

'So the secret's out,' Dan said. 'And what do you think?' he asked his son.

'Good,' Joe said through his cake with a decisive nod of the head. 'It's good.'

By six o'clock we were back home. Dan was cooking dinner and Joe was sitting at the kitchen table, drawing with wax crayons. I pulled out my sketch book and decided to join in.

'Wow, that's really good,' Dan said, having come over to see what we were doing and looked over my shoulder. 'You never told me you could draw,' he continued, his expression still incredulous. 'Joe, have you seen this drawing Hattie did of you?'

'Uh huh,' he nodded.

I let Dan pick it up to take a closer look. I couldn't remember the last time I'd drawn with a wax crayon but I had to admit it had worked well and Joe was such a good subject. Both of his elbows on the table, his shoulders rounded around his work, he had a cute little frown when he was concentrating.

'She did one of you too,' Joe piped up.

'Oh really,' Dan smiled and he noticed my little embarrassed frown before he flicked back a page. He didn't say anything straight away and I watched with my tongue between my teeth as his eyes took it in. Slowly he began to nod and then he looked at me.

'This is really good Hattie.'

'Thanks,' I smiled. I'd drawn him whilst he had been cooking, unaware that I was watching from across the kitchen, noting the angle of his chin, the darkness of his eyes, the gentleness of his hands. When I drew someone I found out so much more about them.

'Can I?' he asked, going to turn back another page.

'Sure,' I said.

I watched his expression as he flicked from one drawing to the next.

'These ones of your cats remind me of Beatrix Potter's drawings,' he said. 'Is that Modi?' he asked,

178

stopping.

I'd drawn Modi a few mornings back as he slept in the armchair and I smiled at the sketch. 'Yes, that's him.'

Dan was quiet for a moment. 'The only thing that worries me...,' he began thoughtfully.

I looked up from the page and studied his face, afraid how his sentence might end.

'...is that you'll never love me as much as you love him.'

My frown broke into a wide grin. 'Are you jealous of my cat?' I exclaimed.

'You say that as if it's a ridiculous notion,' he grinned.

'That's because it is,' I replied, although as I said it I knew that I was actually lying. I loved Dan of course, but I loved Modi just as much in another way. Did I really have to choose between them?

Ollie's phone call meant that I did.

The table was set for dinner, the room saturated with the smell of Cannelloni. Dan had just poured two glasses of wine and a beaker of orange squash when I heard my phone ringing from the depths of my bag. I dug it out, saw on the screen that it was Ollie, and put it to my ear.

'Hello,' I said cheerfully.

'Hattie, hi it's Ollie. Sorry if I'm calling at a bad time.'

'No, that's fine,' I replied.

'It's just that I wouldn't call unless I had to,' he fumbled.

His voice sounded uneasy and the smile fell from my face.

'Ollie what's the matter? Are you okay?'

'Yeah, it's not me. It's one of your cats. I think they're ill.'

My heart started pounding. 'Who? Mona again?'

'No, it's Modi.'

I glanced over at Dan who was helping Joe to wash his hands at the kitchen sink. 'Has he been sick? Because Mona was ill only recently. Perhaps-'

Ollie cut me off. 'No, it's not like that. He's gasping, like he's struggling to breathe. He looks bad.'

Overcome by a sudden light-headedness, I reached out to steady myself and found the windowsill. My mouth was dry but when I tried to swallow it hurt. Dan looked up and seeing me, immediately knew that something was wrong.

'When did this start?' I found myself asking.

'Only this morning,' Ollie replied. 'He was fine yesterday. Perhaps a little quiet but I thought nothing of it.'

I looked at the floor as Dan strode over, his hand reaching for mine which was by then clinging to the tiled windowsill, as though it was all I could do to stop my world from spinning. Joe peered up at me through my hair which had fallen in front of my face, his dark eyes wide and wondering, and I bit my lip as I remembered the rushed goodbye I'd bid Modi. The handful of seconds I'd spared him before walking out of the door. His face in the rear view mirror as I'd driven away.

'Hattie, I don't know what to do,' Ollie said urgently.

'What's up Hattie?' Dan asked firmly.

'Hattie are you still there?'

I pulled my head up. 'Ollie I'm coming back. I'll be there as soon as I can.'

'What's going on?' Dan frowned as I put the phone

down.

'Ollie says Modi's ill. I have to go to him.'

Dan looked shocked. 'Right now? We're just about to eat.'

'I know,' I stammered, 'but...'

'Is it bad?'

My eyes flickered back and forth as I wondered whether even I knew the answer. 'I don't know,' I admitted, 'but Ollie wouldn't call me unless he thought so.'

Dan stared at me for several long moments and must have decided from my set expression that nothing was going to change my mind. 'Give me a few hours and I'll go with you. After we've eaten I could arrange to drop Joe at his mum's.'

I started shaking my head. 'I need to go now.'

We both looked down at Joe when he said, 'Is Modi the cat in the photo?'

I nodded and bit my lip to stop it trembling. 'Stay with Joe,' I smiled weakly.

'You'll be all right?' Dan asked.

'Yeah,' I said and then I looked at the table, set for three and I felt a strong pang of guilt. 'But I'm sorry, for ruining the day...for ruining the weekend.'

'Don't be silly,' Dan said, lifting my chin. 'We've had fun, haven't we Joe?' He looked down at his son who nodded enthusiastically. 'I'll catch you up okay? As soon as I can.'

I stepped forwards and kissed him, whispering a yeah as our lips broke apart. 'I love you.'

'I love you too,' he said. 'And don't worry, everything will be fine. Modi will be fine.'

SEVENTEEN

It was raining by the time I stepped back outside. Large puddles already littered the veterinary car park and looking up at the black clouds hanging heavy overhead, the drops hit my face and joined the tears already streaming from my eyes. I didn't care that within moments I was soaked to the skin. I don't think I really noticed. All I knew was that the cat carrier in my hand was empty and suddenly, so was my heart. I clasped a hand to my chest, my fist tightening around the fabric it found there as my breathing came in deep sharp rasps, tugging at my throat so hard it hurt.

I must have whispered one hundred times *don't leave me*, in Modi's ear. As though it was his choice. But slowly he had slipped away and the delicate halves of my broken heart which he had helped stitch back together, were once again in tatters. It was Modi who had been there for me in the darkest of hours. He had saved me when no one else could. He'd dried my tears and made me smile again and he was the one man in my life I had thought would always be there for me. But suddenly he was gone.

When my phone sprang into life, its ring a great din resonating from my pocket, I pulled it out and through the tears clinging to my eyelashes, saw that it was Dan. All I had to do was press one button. One button and I would hear his voice. But he wasn't what I wanted right now. No one could give me that, and so I pressed cancel and buried the phone back in my pocket.

By the time I reached the main street I was beginning to shiver and the rain showed no signs of slowing down. The road gently bent to the left and as my shop came into sight I saw a car parked outside and a figure looking through the window. It was not unusual to see people after hours peering through the glass, the interior of the shop atmospherically lit with lamps, but although he had his back to me and his shoulders rounded against the weather, I would have recognised the man anywhere.

Sinking even deeper into the dreamlike state which seemed to have enveloped me like a bubble, I crossed the road forgetting to check for traffic and a car pipped me loudly as it had to hit the brakes. I froze and shielded my eyes from the headlights, garish in the gloom. The driver was hidden within the darkness of the car and the rain hammered hard on the bonnet.

'Harriet?'

I looked ahead again to see that Richard had turned around and he was staring at me with wide eyes.

'Jesus, Harriet! Are you all right?'

He rushed out into the road and grabbed my hand. The car pipped again as it drove away and I allowed Richard to lead me to the pavement where we stopped and stared at one another. He was almost as wet as I, his blonde hair flat against his head and rain running down his nose. He was wearing his leather jacket I remembered so well and his blue eyes were looking hard into mine.

'Harriet are you okay?' he asked again.

I wasn't but I nodded nonetheless, unable to back it up with any words, and the worry did not fade from his face.

'What's happened?'

I opened my mouth to speak but his question provoked new tears and suddenly all I wanted was for him to hold me. I buried my face in his chest and closed my eyes as he held me tight, just like he used to, and I felt his hand in my hair and his breath on my face.

'Come on, let's go inside,' he said, taking hold of my shoulders. 'You look freezing.' He tried to steer me towards the shop.

'No,' I refused. 'I need to go home.'

'Okay,' he nodded. 'Then I'll drive you.'

He led me to his car and opened the passenger door and once inside I wiped the rain and the tears on my sleeve. I tried not to look as Richard opened the boot and put the empty cat carrier inside.

We drove home in silence. I stared out of the window as the world was swallowed by the night but was not ignorant of the fact that every few seconds he glanced across at me. When the car rolled to a halt outside the garden gate I met one of those glances and then without a word got out, and so did he. We walked to the front door and when my shaky hands struggled to unlock it, he took the keys from me.

'There you go,' he said gently as he turned the key and then pushed the door open, stepping aside to let me pass.

'Are you coming in?' I asked, my voice sounding unusually feeble, as he hovered on the threshold. I don't know why I asked but it felt the right thing to do.

The room was cold and dark. I flicked on the light and shied away from the glare.

'Ollie's gone?' Richard said as he took a cautious step forward. I knew the last thing he wanted was a run in with one of my brothers.

'Yes, he left this morning. He had to go back to London.' The words came from my mouth but they didn't sound like mine.

There wasn't the usual welcome of cats in the kitchen, as though they hadn't heard us arrive, or if they had they had sensed the mood we brought with us and decided to keep away, and as much as I wanted to see them I didn't get any further than the table where I dropped into a chair. Richard glanced around the kitchen, as though he'd never been there before, and then walked over to the sink where he filled the kettle. There had never been a more appropriate moment for a large comforting mug of tea. When he sat down beside me at the table he handed me a towel and I whispered a small thank you as I took it.

'I'm sorry Hattie,' he said softly as I dabbed my hair. 'About your cat. It was a cat wasn't it?'

I bit my lip and nodded. 'I don't understand...' I began, the words coming out as a whimper and the towel falling. 'He was so young.'

'What happened?' he probed as gently as he could.

I looked up from the table top as he went to reach for my hand but then thought better of it. I frowned as I looked into his eyes, my headache steadily building, and I remembered all of the times I had dreamt of Richard coming back and suddenly here he was. He

185

knew me better than anyone else. We'd shared our ambitions, our fears, our entire lives, for years, and despite what he'd done I still found my words running out to him. I wanted to tell him.

'It was his heart,' I said. 'Ollie called me and I rushed back but...I should have been there. He needed me and I wasn't there.' I felt too tired to be angry but I hated myself. I shouldn't have left him. All I could see when I closed my eyes was my rear-view mirror and Modi in it as I'd driven away. I should have stopped. I should have stopped the car and gone back and never let him go. And now I could never hold him again.

'You can't blame yourself,' Richard said, this time touching my arm. 'You didn't know.'

I wiped at my eyes even as new tears fell. Because I did blame myself. Things might have been different if only... 'If only I hadn't gone,' I said aloud.

'If only,' Richard repeated the two words. 'What an amazing thing hindsight is.'

My head was hurting and the more Richard spoke, the worse it became. I couldn't trust myself to think straight as the exhaustion of the last twenty-four hours began to catch up with me, and taking a deep breath I pushed my chair away from the table.

'I'm going to change,' I eventually murmured. I needed to get out of my wet clothes. I left him in the kitchen and wandered upstairs. Having peeled off my jeans and tossed my wet t-shirt on the floor, I opened the wardrobe and pulled out the comfiest jogging bottoms and jumper I owned and pulled them on, regardless of how I looked. Richard had seen me in them before.

I glanced around for my hairbrush and then spotted it on my chest of drawers but froze before picking it up when I spotted a large photo frame sticking out of my weekender bag that I still hadn't unpacked since rushing back the night before. I crouched down and picked it up and then stared at the photograph of Modi and I that Dan had given me. I clutched it tightly to my chest as I gasped with grief and then numbly wandered over to the bed and sank into the mattress. Tears were still not far away and as I curled into a ball, they bled into the pillow. *I love you Modi, I miss you Modi.* The words circled my head and I wondered if he could hear me. I hoped he could hear me because goodbye had been too painful a word to say back there; my lips had failed to shape it, my breath had failed to whisper it...and even now, as it span in my mind with more resonance than a word had ever carried before, it wielded a hammer which made my heart thud.

Goodbye Modi, goodbye.

It was morning when I woke. My eyes were sore and for a moment I couldn't remember why, but then it all rushed back and hit me, like a tidal wave of sorrow. I'd fallen asleep on top of the duvet and someone...Richard...had been in and draped a blanket over me. The air was chilly and I kept the blanket clasped around my shoulders as I climbed to my feet and staggered to the window. His car was still parked outside which meant he was still here. It was early, not even seven o'clock, but I didn't want more sleep. My head had stopped hurting whilst I'd slept but already the ache was back and slowly I made my way downstairs. I still needed that mug of tea.

He was asleep on the sofa. I stood in the living room doorway, my hand clutching the frame, my heart wanting to walk in but my head saying no. He'd draped his wet jeans over the back of a chair, his jacket too. His skin looked pale in the grey morning light trickling through the window and his hair was longer than he ever used to let it grow. He never used to like how it went curly.

I dropped my eyes and turned for the kitchen. Bea was waiting for me, sitting on the tiled floor, and before I could whisper a greeting, for a whisper was all I could seem to muster, my eyes glistened over again.

'How are you little one?' I mumbled as she trotted over and vigorously rubbed her nose against my leg. She looked so much like her brother, only smaller; they'd even had the same little kink at the end of their tails. I picked her up and held her to my chest and she stretched her neck so that her small pink nose touched mine.

'I love you Bea,' I whispered. 'You know that don't you?' It was starting to hurt in the back of my throat again. 'Where's everyone else?'

I looked around the kitchen. First I spotted Mona, sitting quietly under one of the chairs. Then Flicks stepped out of her hiding place behind the shoe rack. Lastly Coco appeared, staring solemnly at me through a gap in the curtains. I crouched down and beckoned them over, reaching out to stroke each of them on the head. Suddenly we were down to the five of us and it seemed such a small, sorry number. I poured out their breakfast and then stared at the surplus bowl at the end of the line. And then the sluice gate opened.

Sitting on a bench, hugging my knees to my chest, I was looking out across my favourite view but as the tears built up in my eyes and then began to run down my face, all I could see was a blur where something so beautiful had once been. When my heart had broken before it had hurt more than I'd ever known was possible, but this time around it was different. I felt empty, so empty I couldn't be sick even though I felt ill to my core. There were no restraints anymore. I was alone. No one was there to see me weep, and so I sat and let myself be consumed by my grief.

Eventually I tired. My shoulders stopped shaking and I took great gulps of air to replenish my lungs.

'Hattie?'

I span around and saw that it was Richard.

'You okay?' he asked.

I roughly wiped my eyes and nodded. 'How did you know where I was?'

He sat down next to me. 'This is your favourite spot. Did you think I'd forgotten?'

The small smile I found felt alien and neither of us said anything else for a while, we just sat and gazed at the view.

'I suppose you think I'm being silly, crying over a cat,' I finally said.

'No,' Richard smiled. 'I knew the girl I married had a heart of gold.'

I glanced across at him, wondering if he knew how much he was killing me. 'I'm guessing you're not here about your guitar,' I said.

'I'm sorry about that,' he replied, looking awkward. 'The first time I rang I couldn't even say hello, I just hung up. The second time I still couldn't admit why I was calling; I had to think of something.' He paused and his eyes searched my face. 'But everything else I said on the phone...it was true. I am sorry. And then when you told me to stop calling...' He sighed and ran a hand through his hair. 'I needed to see you again Hattie. I had to speak to you.'

He stopped then and looked at me as though waiting for an answer but as far as I was concerned he hadn't asked a question, just hinted at one.

'We're talking now,' I said. 'What is it you want?'

'Don't you know?' he replied.

I closed my eyes and shook my head. 'I'm tired of trying to work you out Richard. I thought we were happy. Look how wrong I was there. Don't make me guess the questions you aren't brave enough to ask. Can't you just say it? Tell me straight.'

He looked almost wounded by the sharpness of my tone and visibly took a deep breath as his gaze ran to the horizon and then back.

'I want you back Hattie. There, that's the truth. I should never have left.'

It was one thing to expect it, another to hear him say it and just as my eyes were drying up they threatened tears again. I looked up at the sky and tried to hold them back. I could hear a blackbird singing in the hedgerow and up above a kestrel was drifting like a feather on a current of air.

'What do you think?' I heard Richard say, a slight quiver in his voice.

'You're a jerk,' I suddenly spat and rushed to my feet.

'Wait, Hattie! Please!' he shouted, running after me and pulling me back, his fingers locked tightly around my arm. 'Hear me out?'

'You cheated on me Richard!' I cried, trying to push him away. 'With my best friend of all people. How can I forgive that?'

'It's over,' he insisted, holding onto my arm no

matter how hard I pushed him away. 'I haven't seen her in weeks.'

'Did she grow tired of you?' I asked disdainfully.

'I left her!'

'So you got bored and you think you can just come back here? Give me a little respect Richard!'

'It's not like that,' he started.

'Isn't it? Isn't that what you do?

'No,' he tried to argue but I didn't want to hear it.

'Do you really think it can ever be the same again between us?' I asked. 'You broke your promise. You broke my heart. Do you know what that feels like?'

'I do now,' he said quietly. 'Because I'm still in love with you. I've always loved you. I think I always will.'

With those words I was rendered weak. I couldn't hate him, I didn't have the strength anymore. I thought to myself that I should feel empowered. He wanted me and suddenly the ball was in my court but I was exhausted, drained, too tired to think straight.

'You know,' I eventually said, 'night after night I lay awake, imagining this moment. I never thought it would ever come true but here you are.' I shrugged and shook my head. 'The only part of it I never anticipated was that you would be too late.'

'Too late?' he frowned. 'Why? You mean you've met someone else?'

I stayed silent and he correctly read that as a yes.

'Is it serious?'

I heard myself laugh, an unhappy, bitter laugh. 'You're talking like this is my fault but you're the one who left me, remember?'

'And it was the biggest mistake of my life! You're right, I am a jerk. In fact I've been a fucking asshole. But I swear to you, right now, that I'm sorry. I mean it.'

I shut my eyes as my headache continued to build behind them. 'This is not just something I can decide in a heartbeat Richard,' I said. 'I've moved on, I don't know if I can walk back into this again. I don't even know if I want to.'

'What's his name?'

I stared at him and wondered whether he was serious. 'It doesn't matter,' I said.

'It matters to me,' he replied brusquely.

'Why?'

'Does he know you like I do?' he asked. 'Does he hold you like I did?'

'Richard please...'

'Do you remember our first anniversary,' he interrupted, 'when we went to the mountains?'

I licked a tear from my lip and nodded.

'I'd never been happier.' Richard reached for my hand and held it. 'I've missed you so much,' he whispered, pulling me closer, and this time I didn't resist. 'I was an idiot and I'm sorry,' he said as he slipped one arm around my waist, then brushed the tears from my face with his other hand. 'Do you think you can ever forgive me?'

I closed my eyes. My head was pulsing and I could hear my heartbeat in my ears. Our lips only a breadth apart, the warmth of his breath was gentle on my face. I began to melt in his arms, and then he kissed me.

Stop! What are you doing? I heard my conscience scream and I pulled back. 'I can't Richard,' I said, shaking my head. 'I can't do this.'

'Hattie, please,' he whispered. 'Give me another chance.'

I knew that I should have said no. I should have told him to leave. But deep down inside there was a part of me that thought differently. The part of me that had always wanted him. That had always needed him. That still loved him. I'd managed to lock it away, keep it out of sight, but Richard knew it was still there and all he had to do was find it.

'Hattie, please? Just one more chance?'

EIGHTEEN

I'd been staring into the bottom of an empty wine glass when the phone started ringing and slowly I lifted my head and looked across the living room. The evening was cool and the house sat in darkness, my thoughts having locked me in a dream-like state since the sun had begun to fall behind the horizon. Reluctantly I climbed off the sofa and switched on a table lamb before answering the phone.

'Hello?'

'Hattie, it's me.'

Already I felt queasy, just hearing Dan's voice, queasy with guilt because of the thoughts that had been circling my head.

'How are you?' he asked.

He wanted to know about Modi, if he was okay, if I'd made it in time.

'Not good,' I replied, trying my best to control the waver in my voice.

'Oh God Hattie,' he said, knowing what my simple

194

reply had meant. 'I'm so sorry.'

I tried to say something then but the words dried up and died before I could even shape them. I wondered if he could hear me sniffing back tears and told myself to stop; be strong.

'I'm going to come over.'

'No,' I said. 'No you don't have to, I'll be all right.'

'But what if I want to,' Dan replied.

'I think...'

'What?' Dan prompted as my sentence faded.

'I think what I need right now is some time to myself,' I told him. 'I just need time, okay? Time to get my head straight.'

'You could always come here,' Dan suggested. 'You could forget about it and be here with me.'

'I don't want to forget about him Dan.'

'Of course not,' he replied. 'I didn't mean it like that Hattie. I just meant that maybe I could help,' Dan said. 'I want to help you.'

I took a deep breath and tried to calm myself down. 'I just need to be alone. There's a lot of stuff going on at the moment and I'm trying to work it out.'

There was a pause but then I heard Dan mutter some kind of agreement. 'Is Ollie still there?' he asked.

'No,' I said.

'Then who was there with you this morning?'

My heart began to pound fiercely. 'What do you mean?'

'I rang this morning,' he said. 'A guy picked up, he said you were busy and put the phone down.'

Richard, that jerk, I thought, clenching my teeth.

'Oh that must have been Ollie,' I lied quickly. 'He left this afternoon. He didn't tell me you'd called.'

'He sounded kind of mad at me.'

'Mad?' I repeated.

There was a long pause and I began to worry that Dan knew more than he was letting on.

'Should I be worried Harriet?' Dan asked. 'Are we okay here? I get the feeling something's going on with you.'

I didn't reply straight away and that was my mistake because then it didn't matter what I said, the sincerity was not there. 'I'm fine. We're fine,' I told him but I was lying and he could tell too even if he didn't say so. The truth was I kept wondering, if I hadn't rushed off to be with Dan, if I been here and gotten Modi help sooner, could he have been saved? The vet had said probably not, and that 'probably', that ounce of uncertainty, was what haunted me. I was angry with myself and ultimately with Dan too, because I'd fallen so madly in love with him.

'I have to go,' I lied.

'Can I call you tomorrow?' he asked.

'Yeah, of course,' I replied, wondering if my tone contradicted me. 'I'll speak to you tomorrow.'

'I love you Hattie,' he said.

'You too.'

I put the phone down and went back to the sofa where a photo album I'd dug out of the bottom of the closet, was lying open. I had considered burning it on more than one occasion since the day Richard had left but all of the memories it held were too dear to me to lose.

'Shit,' I said aloud. I had so much thinking to do.

Charlie had the morning off and I'd been drifting around the shop all morning, aware of all the jobs that needed doing but unable to settle on any of them. If I wasn't thinking of Richard, I was thinking of Dan, and all the while I tried not to think of Modi but the harder I tried the more I failed. I took the lid off a tin of wax polish and sighed as I looked at the wardrobe that needed attending to; No one was going to buy it unless it looked its best, but realising I'd left the cloth back in the office I didn't have the strength to fetch it and so I just sat, staring at the wood, my eyes tracing the grain. My heart was getting tired of being split three ways and I seemed unable to function as the cracks deepened.

When the doorbell rang it made me jump but it gave me an excuse to abandon the polishing and so I stood up and headed for the stairs.

'Richard,' I said, my footsteps faltering several treads from the bottom as I realised who it was.

He smiled at me and awkwardly I tucked my hair behind my ear, hoping I looked better than I felt.

'How are you?' he asked.

I didn't want to admit I felt dreadful so claimed that I wasn't bad. 'What are you doing here?' I said, making it to the bottom of the stairs and reaching for the desk where my fingertips clung to the wood as though it was a raft and I lost out at sea.

'I just wanted to see you,' he admitted and took a cautious step towards me.

'I told you I'd think about it Richard. I'm still thinking.'

'I know, I know,' he replied hurriedly. 'I understand.'

'And I heard about the phone call,' I told him, wondering how he would react. 'That didn't help your case.'

His smile vanished.

'Why did you do that?' I asked. 'Why didn't you tell me?'

'Why do you think?' he replied. 'I've already told you I love you and then some guy calls your house.' He was frowning, the hurt etched into his face. 'I was jealous okay? I hate to think that someone else loves you too.'

I nodded, seeing his point, and as I looked away he took another step in my direction.

'I got you something.' He took a small blue box from his pocket. 'Open it,' he said as I hesitated.

'Richard I don't-'

'Hattie it's not a bribe,' he interrupted, smiling again. 'I just want you to have it.'

Eventually I took it from him and tried not to look too aghast when I opened it. Inside was a beautiful bracelet. I didn't want to know how much it cost and I was torn between thanking him and giving it back when the doorbell rang again and a man walked in.

'Morning,' I smiled at the customer before turning and heading for the office. Richard followed and closed the door behind us.

'Richard-'

'Like I said it's not a bribe Harriet,' he interrupted again. 'I used to give you presents all the time.'

'Yes but we were married then,' I reminded him.

'Look, what are you doing tomorrow night?' he asked.

'I'm busy,' I lied and suspected he knew it too.

'Then when can I see you?'

I sighed, hating the pressure he was mounting up on me. 'I'll call you,' I said.

'Okay,' he nodded, and smiled, then reached for my hand and gave it a little squeeze. 'I'll see you soon then?'

'Yeah,' I replied, finding a small smile too.

His eyes lingered on my face for a moment and then he turned for the door. 'I love you,' he said and then he was gone.

I sank into a chair and looked at the bracelet again and that was where Charlie found me.

'What's that?' she asked, taking off her jacket and draping it over the back of a chair.

'Oh, er-' I stammered, snapping the lid shut. 'Just a bracelet. How are you?'

She grinned and ignored my question. 'Who from?'

'Dan,' I fibbed, relieved that she hadn't arrived a few minutes earlier and seen Richard leave.

'When do I get to meet this Dan?' she asked, taking the box off me. 'Wow,' she exclaimed, her jaw dropping as she looked at the bracelet and then back at me. 'You're one lucky girl,' she smiled.

I tried to smile too but couldn't.

'What's up?' Charlie frowned, suddenly aware something was wrong.

I heaved a sigh and looked down at my hands. 'I had a bad weekend Charlie,' I admitted.

Instantly she was alert, afraid. 'What happened?'

Already the pain was back, tugging maliciously at my throat. 'It was Modi,' I struggled.

She clasped her hands to her mouth, knowing what I was about to say because suddenly my eyes were swimming with tears.

'He died.' I turned away and tried to catch the tears before they made tracks. 'I'm sorry,' I spluttered.

'No, no, don't be. It's okay, I understand.' She pulled over a spare chair and sat down next to me, enveloping me in a hug. 'I'm so sorry,' she said, holding me tightly and the tears continued to fall.

I wanted so much to tell her everything, about Richard, about the battle going on inside of me; It was so painful to keep it to myself and yet I daren't because

I knew what she would think. She would say just the same as everyone else I daren't tell; my sister, my parents. They would say that Richard didn't deserve a second chance and I knew that too, but then why was it that I wanted to give it another try?

'Where's Dan now?' Charlie asked. 'Is he here?'

I shook my head.

'No? Why not?' she frowned.

'I told him not to come,' I explained.

'Why did you do that?'

I just shrugged. 'It's complicated.'

'Complicated? What's so complicated?'

I didn't elaborate and so she continued.

'He loves you Harriet. I've never met him but I only need to look at that bracelet to know that. I think you could do with some support right now,' Charlie said, 'so just call him and say you've changed your mind. He'd be here in a heartbeat!'

Despite Charlie's best intentions, this conversation wasn't helping. My stomach was knotting up with the anticipation of disaster and I just wondered how much longer the fuse had to burn.

NINETEEN

I wasn't sleeping much. Dan had called that evening, as he'd said he would, but I'd let it go to voicemail and not rung back. Now it was four in the morning and I lay staring at the ceiling, wondering what it was I would say when he called again. Did I really want to end it with him for Richard? Eventually I was dragged into an uneasy sleep and woke again not long before six, and by then I was so sick of tossing and turning in my sheets that I got up and headed to the bathroom for a shower.

'Shit!' I cried as the water came out ice cold. If I hadn't been wide awake before I certainly was now and I hurried to turn off the tap before leaping back out of the shower. 'That's just great,' I muttered as, huddled in a towel, I tried the sink tap but again nothing but cold water came out.

Just after lunch I left the shop in Charlie's hands and headed to a hardware shop where I found myself in an aisle confronted with new boilers.

'Harriet?'

I looked sharply to the right as I heard someone say my name.

'What are you doing here?' Richard smiled as he walked over.

'What are you doing here?' I asked back, my heart beating fast. It was a stupid question; He was an electrician after all.

'Just getting some things for a job I'm working on,' he replied. He looked so pleased to see me.

'Oh,' I muttered.

'What are you looking at boilers for?' he asked.

'I think mine's packed in,' I said quietly, looking away from him. 'It's stopped working.'

'You might not need a new one. Want me to take a look at it?' he offered.

'No, no,' I replied.

'Why not?' he said. His voice was so warm, his eyes so kind. 'I might be able to fix it. It's no trouble.'

'You're busy,' I said.

'I can come after work.'

'I don't know about that,' I told him, shaking my head.

'Don't worry Harriet. I get it, you're still thinking. It's not a date, I'm just offering to help you out.'

He raised his eyebrows as I thought about it.

'Look, I'm working over your way,' he said. 'I'll call in on the way home, I'll take a look at the boiler, then leave...if that's what you want.'

'Okay,' I eventually agreed.

He smiled. 'Good.'

'But this doesn't change anything,' I reiterated.

'I know,' he said. 'I'll be there around six, okay?'

I nodded. 'See you then.'

'Did you speak to Dan?' Charlie asked as we closed up.

'Not yet,' I said, not meeting her eye. 'I will tonight.'

She picked up her jacket but fell short of pulling it on. 'Are you sure there's nothing else on your mind Harriet? You seem so quiet.'

'There's nothing,' I said, shaking my head.

'You look... I don't know, worried...almost scared.'

I was scared. I was scared because I'd made up my mind, somewhere during that long afternoon. I had made my decision at last and now came the hard part; Tonight I would have to tell him.

'I'm fine, honestly,' I told her. 'I just feel a little under the weather. I'll be better tomorrow.'

She nodded, reassured by that, and then said goodbye.

Richard was there at six, as he'd promised, and I watched from the kitchen window as he climbed out of his van. It was strange seeing him walk up the garden path as though he was coming home from work.

'Hi,' he smiled as I opened the door.

'Hi,' I said back.

Time seemed to stop as we gazed at one another but eventually I broke the link. 'Richard, I-'

'It's okay, I know where the boiler is,' he interrupted.

'No, wait,' I said. 'I need to talk to you.'

His smile disappeared as he realised he was about to get the answer he'd been waiting for.

I wrung my hands, finding it hard to pick the right words but then something happened I had not expected; A car pulled up outside the gate. My eyes widened and I began to panic as I realised it was Dan.

'Oh God,' I said quietly.

Seeing my expression, Richard turned around. 'Who's that?' he asked as Dan climbed out of the car.

My lips opened but I didn't know what to say, my heart pounding against my ribs as though there was a stampede of wildebeest circling my chest.

Dan had his hand on the gate before he saw us and as soon as his eyes met mine and he read the guilt all over my face, he froze.

I glanced at Richard and found that he was studying me. 'Is that-?'

'Yes,' I answered prematurely. 'Shit!' I cursed and brushed past him. 'Dan?' I said as I approached the gate.

Dan was looking at me, then over my shoulder and back again. 'Sorry, I didn't realise you had company,' he said a little coldly.

'This isn't what it looks like,' I told him, trying to reach for his hand but he pulled away.

'Are you sure?' he asked, his voice saturated with scepticism. 'Who is that? Or do you want me to guess?' I'd never seen him angry or upset before, and suddenly I was faced with a concoction of both.

I bit my lip as it began to waver and tried to fight the urge to look anywhere else but into his eyes. 'It's Richard,' I said.

The lines in his forehead deepened. 'Your ex-husband?'

I nodded and so did he, as though it was the answer he'd been expecting, and his hands on his hips, he looked away from me. I followed his line of sight and suddenly realised that Mrs Ellis was in her front garden, holding a small watering can in a pathetic attempt to disguise the fact that she was snooping. If she was hoping for a show, the chances were pretty good that she was going to get one because Richard had followed me down the path.

Dan looked back at me. 'And I'm supposed to believe that he just nipped round for-'

'Back off pal,' Richard interrupted him. 'I don't know what you think you're doing just turning up out of the blue but this has got nothing to do with you.'

'Richard, please, stop it,' I asked, manoeuvring my way between them.

'What are you talking about? It's got everything to do with me,' Dan replied, glaring back.

'If Harriet had wanted you here, I think she would have asked you,' Richard said. 'And by the looks of it she didn't ask you.'

'Richard, please! Can you just give us a minute?' I cried.

The situation was deteriorating fast and I so desperately wanted to hit rewind as my life spiralled out of control. At this rate I could sense it turning into a full-blown punch-up and by the looks of it so did Mrs Ellis. The arm holding the watering can had fallen inanimately to her side. She wasn't even pretending anymore, just gaping, relishing her front row seat.

'Nothing's happened here,' I told Dan.

'Then what's he doing here?' he asked.

'Just talking.'

'About what?' Dan said.

When I didn't answer straight away, Richard felt the need to fill in. 'About getting back together,' he said.

'What?' I said, spinning round to look at Richard. 'I mean, well yeah, but I hadn't given him my answer yet,' I assured Dan.

Dan took another step away from me, recoiling as

though from a bullet. 'And what was that going to be, just before I turned up?' he asked.

My mouth fell open and I glanced at Richard. I hadn't wanted to do it like this. Despite how our marriage had ended, I'd loved him once and to see him hurt, hurt me as well. I recalled our past with a warm glow in my heart but I now knew that we had no future.

'You know what?' Dan said. 'I don't want you to even answer that. It's easier if I don't hear it.'

'No Dan, you don't understand,' I cried. I yanked the gate open and rushed after him as he headed for his car. 'I was going to turn him down,' I said, reaching for his arm.

He pulled away and shook his head. 'I don't believe you.'

'Please you have to! I don't love him anymore. At first I thought I did but-'

'You slept with him just to make sure?'

It was my turn to be shocked and I stared at him as though he was crazy. 'No!' I cried. 'Of course not! Do you really think I'd do that?'

'I saw your face when I arrived Harriet. You looked guilty as hell!'

'I did feel guilty,' I replied, 'I still do, but not for that reason.'

'Then why?' he said angrily.

'I felt guilty for even considering of walking away from everything we have. I didn't know you were coming. I never wanted you two to meet, but only so that you would never know that for even one second I'd doubted us.'

Dan looked away and leant against the car.

'I was unhappy,' I mumbled. 'I was grieving. I know that's no excuse but I wasn't thinking straight.'

He sighed and ran a hand through his hair. 'You know what Harriet? I was always there for you. I would have come, I offered, remember?'

I licked a tear from my lip but my eyes were brimming with more to follow. 'I know,' I said.

'Can you answer me one more question?' he asked, his voice lowering to almost a whisper.

'Anything,' I nodded, my eyes pleading with him to stay.

'Was it really Ollie who picked up the phone yesterday morning?'

My heart plummeted, as though someone had ripped it out of my chest and let it sink to the ocean's depths. Answering truthfully was like a death sentence. Dan would never believe that all Richard and I had done was talk if he'd answered my home phone early in the morning. But I couldn't lie any longer. He could read the truth on my face.

'No,' I said, gently shaking my head. 'It wasn't Ollie.'

'You were just talking then too huh? All night.' Dan said, drawing to his conclusions and making up his mind. His eyes had a sheen to them but he wouldn't cry.

'I never cheated, I swear,' I whispered. 'I'm sorry.'

'Don't be,' Dan said. 'You chose him. I hope you're happy.'

'But I didn't,' I wept. 'I chose you.'

He turned away and opened the car door.

'Please don't leave,' I said softly, reaching for his hand but he clenched it into a fist.

'Why?' he frowned, his voice cold. 'So you can promise me what you've just promised him?'

'I haven't promised him anything.'

'Please don't Hattie,' he said quietly. 'I've heard

enough.' He reached into the car and picked something up. 'By the way you left this,' he said, pushing my sketch book into my hand. 'Joe made you something. It's inside.'

I stared down numbly at the sketch book and he got in the car.

'Goodbye Harriet,' he said, swallowing hard, and then he was gone.

I stood rooted to the spot, paralysed with shock. It was over, just like that. Slowly I opened the sketch book and tucked inside the cover was a drawing from Joe. I bit my lip as it began to tremble when my eyes wandered across the paper. It was a picture of us; Dan, Joe and I aboard the boat, a small ginger cat at my feet. Only a couple of days ago that had been me, all the pieces of the jigsaw at last in place. How catastrophically it had all fallen apart.

I wanted to disappear, to sink into the sofa and cry out my heart. I wanted to find Bea, Mona, Flicks and Coco and hold them tight. And most of all I wanted Modi. But when I eventually turned around I remembered that I had broken two hearts in the last five minutes and Richard was still stood in the garden. The bravado gone, he stared at me like I'd slapped him across the face.

Brushing the hair from my face and swiping at my tears, I walked up to him. 'I'm sorry,' I said softly. 'I didn't want you to hear that.'

He didn't say anything, just looked at the ground.

'I want you to know that I really thought about it,' I eventually said, hoping he'd find some comfort in that.

'But you choose him?' he asked.

I nodded.

'Even though he just walked away?'

I tried to swallow the lump in my throat but it wouldn't budge. 'Yes,' I said, stumbling over the word. I reached into my pocket then and felt for the bracelet.

'Here,' I said, giving it back.

'No,' Richard shook his head. 'Keep it, something to remember me by.' He was about to turn away when he hesitated. 'Just for the record,' he added, 'I hope you remember that I realised my mistake, even if I was too late.'

'I won't forget,' I whispered.

I watched him walk back to his van, but called his name as he opened the door. 'Richard?'

He lifted his head and looked back.

'Goodbye Richard,' I said, managing a small smile.

He dipped his chin in acknowledgement and for a moment we gazed at one another, our eyes relaying an unspoken final farewell, because no matter what, neither of us would ever forget all of those days and all of those nights that we had spent together. As husband and wife. As best friends.

TWENTY

It was only work which kept my head above the waves of the storm that followed. My workshop became my world and if I kept my mind focused, didn't let my thoughts wander from the task at hand, I knew I might be able to claw my way out of the dark someday. I'd given up on ever hearing from Dan again when he didn't answer what felt like my hundredth thousandth call. It had been two weeks. He'd had time to cool off, to think about it, but still he didn't want to talk. Charlie said not to give up, that he'd come around in the end, but I knew it was over.

I closed early one Friday afternoon and called at a garden centre on the way home. I was stood in front of the roses when a young girl who worked there asked if she could help me. Startled out of my reverie, I looked across at her.

'Err, yes, I'm looking for a rose but...' I broke off and shook my head. 'I don't know which to pick.'

'Well...' the girl said, 'Is it for you?'

'It's kind of a gift,' I replied, looking back at the roses in the hope that she wouldn't see that my eyes were swimming.

'Your husband?' she asked.

'No, no,' I said, shaking my head again. 'A friend, a good friend. One that I love very much...and miss.'

The girl stepped up to the roses, biting her lip as she thought about it. 'What about this one?' she said. It was a climber, the pearly white petals gently clustered around the heart of each flower.

I stared at it and then looked at her with a thankful smile. 'It's perfect.'

When I got home I found my gardening trowel amongst the geraniums. I hadn't remembered putting it there but then again, so many days just lately seemed to go by in a blur. I dug a hole near the hedge, next to the small gap through which Modi always left the garden. Once I'd planted the rose I knelt on the grass, my hands clasped in my lap, and then closed my eyes as I remembered all of those times when he had looked up at me with wide yellow eyes, asking to be held. I'd whisk him up in my arms and feel the gentle beating of his heart close to mine and I was still struggling to accept that that would never happen again. He wouldn't be sitting in the armchair when I walked in, looking back at me across the room. He wouldn't try and sneak into my bedroom when I wasn't looking and curl up on the pillows. But he was still here, I could feel it, and my heart could at least rest knowing that the kitten I'd found in a cardboard box had lived a happy life.

My eyes shot open when I felt something small and cold touch the back of my hand. It was Bea's nose and reaching out, I stroked her head.

'Hello little one,' I smiled. I picked her up and then

heard a car stop outside the gate. I glanced over my shoulder from my hiding place as my parents got out of their car and then looking back down at Bea, I held her a little tighter. I didn't want to go, I wanted to stay here, with her, with the others. No false smiles, no having to make conversation, but I had no choice. Lou had put a lot of effort into this surprise party and I had to make sure my mum arrived at the right moment. I climbed to my feet and met my parents in the garden around the front of the house.

'Hello there Harriet, ready to go?' my dad smiled cheerily, but when he spotted my grubby hands and jeans, I felt that they said no for me.

His face fell into the same concerned frown he had worn the last couple of times we'd spoken but my mum kept her smile and hugged me tight. My face in her shoulder, she smelt of lavender, and my heart started to beat faster as I clung to her, feeling as vulnerable as the child I'd once been.

'Happy birthday mum,' I said as I peeled away from her.

'Thank you Harriet,' she smiled. She was wearing what looked like a new dress and she looked happy, excited even, and suddenly I felt guilty for not feeling the same. 'I've packed,' I lied. 'I've just got to change but I won't take long.'

'That's okay, we've got time,' my mum reassured me. 'Lou said to be there by six didn't she?'

I nodded. She thought we were heading to Lou's for a meal. In fact neither of them knew that actually over thirty guests would be there.

We went inside and leaving them in the kitchen, I disappeared upstairs. Quickly I changed into some fresh clothes, jeans and a simple pullover; I didn't have the energy to try any harder. I dug my weekender bag out of the bottom of the wardrobe and filled it with enough things to last me an overnight stay. In the bathroom I picked up my toiletries and spared a moment to look in the mirror. The eyes that stared back at me were dull and some mud had found its way onto my cheek. I washed it off and then rubbed my face with a towel, sighing as I hid from my reflection. When I felt strong enough to take a second look I realised my hair looked as unhappy as my face, and so grabbed my brush and did what I could. When I trundled back downstairs I found my dad in the living room, hunched over something at my desk. It was my sketch book. I remembered leaving it open on the drawing of Dan. When my dad realised I was beside him, he cleared his throat and stood up straight.

'Ready?' he asked, turning away from the sketch book without a word about it.

'Almost,' I said. 'You can head to the car, I'll be there in a moment.'

'All right,' he replied. He took my bag and together with my mum, headed outside.

Alone with the girls in the kitchen, I crouched down and stroked each of them.

'I promise I won't be gone long, okay fellas? It's just one night. Everything will be okay.' Bea, Mona, Flicks and Coco stared back at me. If I was honest, the words tumbling out of my mouth were a last attempt to reassure me. It was difficult. I was scared of returning to find I'd lost another and I could think of little else. I topped up their food again, even though they already had plenty to last them, and then hesitated before reaching down and picking up Modi's bowl. My knuckles turned white as I clutched it tightly in both hands and then I hid it in the dark depths of the pantry.

'See you tomorrow,' I said, trying a smile as the girls lapped at a plate of milk, and then I walked out of the door.

The journey was a quiet one, the atmosphere in the car melancholic. My parents made a few noteworthy attempts to rouse me into conversation but I didn't have the heart to keep any from petering out. It wasn't that I didn't want to be amiable. I hated the silences as much as they did but it felt so hard to be that person I used to be. Gazing out of the window I began to wonder whether it had been worth me coming at all for the company I was and I was forced to prolong their suffering when Lou sent me a text. *Can you stall them for fifteen minutes, not ready*, it said.

We were only five minutes away, driving through her local town, and it was tricky to convince my parents that I was so suddenly desperate for the loo and just couldn't wait until we got there. They frowned at me over their shoulders like I was still strapped in a toddler's seat and I didn't thank Lou for making me look so childish. My dad stopped the car and as he pointed out a sign for the public toilets, I hopped out.

'You might as well stretch your legs, have a walk round,' I said. 'See you back here in fifteen minutes, yeah?'

'We can't, we'll be late,' my mum replied.

'It's okay, Lou won't mind.' Before they could insist against it, I set off in the direction of the toilets but once out of sight I changed course and wandered up the high street. The shops were shut but I was content to gaze through the windows, hesitating the longest outside an antique shop. An elegant Louis the sixteenth style chair stood just the other side of the glass, reupholstered in green silk, and beside that a round table with barley sugar legs. But what caught my eye most was what sat on top of that. My own gramophone was still at home, sitting quietly in the corner of the living room. It was better than the one I was looking at and would fetch a good price, but to sell it would be to fully accept that Dan was never coming back and despite everything, a very small flame of hope still flickered somewhere in the depths of my heart.

When I returned to the car I was met with two very serious glares.

'Get lost did you?' my mum frowned.

'I thought we agreed fifteen minutes?' I said, climbing back in.

My dad looked at me in the rear view mirror as he turned the key, with that look he often used when he thought I was being awkward, and I found myself muttering an apology. Definitely should have stayed at home, I thought to myself as I fastened my seatbelt and we set off again.

Lou and Tom had a large detached mock-Tudor house and out the front sat her red mini on the brick forecourt which had been a lawn the last time I'd visited. The evening was warm and the trees lively with the chatter of songbirds as we got out of the car. My mum rang the doorbell and we waited, then rang again when no one came.

'It's very quiet,' my dad frowned.

'Yes,' my mum seconded, looking concerned. 'Do you think she's forgotten we're coming?'

'Her car's here,' my dad said.

'Perhaps she's round the back,' I suggested, knowing full well she was.

Together we walked around the side of the house via a flagstone path and as soon as we stepped onto the tightly clipped back lawn, everyone leapt from their hiding places.

'Surprise!'

My mum clasped both hands to her mouth and for a moment, as her eyes danced around the garden full of familiar faces all staring at her, I wasn't sure whether she was going to laugh or cry.

'Happy birthday,' Lou beamed as she rushed forwards. The look of shock on my mum's face did not fade and Lou reached for her hand. 'Say something,' she smiled.

My mum's mouth opened then closed a few times but eventually she managed to splutter, 'Wow,' and a wave of laughter circled the garden. 'Thank you, I...I can't believe it. I had no idea...' My mum broke off and her eyes began welling up with tears.

'Are these good tears or bad tears?' Lou asked.

'Good tears,' my mum smiled, reaching for a tissue. 'It's wonderful, it really is. Thank you Lou. It's so great to see everyone. Hello Chris, hello Ollie,' she beamed as her two youngest sons stepped up. She hugged them both and then Ryan edged his way to the front too. Before she knew it my mum was swamped with hugs and happy birthday wishes and with all the commotion I found myself being ushered further and further back. I watched their faces, glowing with smiles, and wished I could be one of them.

Lou really had put everything into the party. It looked fantastic, down to the last detail. There were candles and flowers on every linen tablecloth. Garlands hanging overhead danced in the gentle evening breeze and small white lights shimmered from the trees. She'd even hired a band and when she nodded her head they began to play, kicking off with my mum's favourite song which only made her smile grow. There was a light in her eyes I had not seen for a long time and I knew now that Lou had been right to throw her the party. I recognised most of the faces as they laughed and chatted. All of my siblings were there, my mum's sister Lucy and her brother Grahame too. Nephews, nieces, cousins and old friends, I watched them all from afar, struggling to join in, Will particularly catching my eye as he introduced a girl to my parents I had never seen before.

Eventually I slipped from the crowd in search of a drink. Beneath a gazebo I found what I was looking for and poured myself a large glass of rosé, then took a sip as I looked back across the garden. Lou was still fussing around mum, making sure everything was as perfect as she'd planned but then suddenly, with a frown on her face, she began looking around as though she had lost something. She turned to the person beside her and asked them a question but they just shrugged, and her eyes narrowed further as her search became more desperate. I knew it was me she was looking for when at last our eyes met across the busy lawn and she came to an abrupt halt, but I barely held the gaze for more than a moment before turning away. I didn't feel like making conversation but unfortunately for me I ran straight into Aunt Lucy, and she always did.

'Hello there Harriet, how are your foxgloves this year?' she beamed. Aunt Lucy was a bubbly woman, tall and a little eccentric. She taught English literature for a living but her heart was in gardening, hence the question.

'Fine thanks Lucy,' I smiled back.

She'd only visited my house the once and been, as she put it, gobsmacked by the garden.

'You're very talented Harriet,' she had told me at the time, and ever since she had reiterated those words each time we met, with today being no exception.

'I particularly loved that little seating area you'd made,' she said, 'and then there was that beautiful stone urn,' she added, 'that you'd got lavender in. You've certainly got the eye.'

'Thank you,' I said.

'I tried some lavender myself this year but it's not doing too good. I knew it was optimistic to try, the ground's too rich for it.'

I nodded in comprehension and took another sip of wine as she surged on.

'Mind you, Louise must have green fingers too by the looks of this place. It's immaculate.'

In fact Lou's input went as far as hiring the gardener but not wanting to disappoint Aunt Lucy, I didn't say so.

'What a fantastic job she's made of this party, don't you think?'

I nodded again. 'Yes, it's lovely.'

'And where's your man? David is it? No Dan,' she corrected herself with a smile. 'I haven't seen him yet. Your mum told me all about him.'

'Actually we broke up,' I told her and prayed she didn't ask for further details.

'Oh,' she said, her face crumpling in pity. 'Never mind, no man's worth the heartache anyway in my opinion.'

Aunt Lucy had been divorced three times but seemed to come out of it empowered rather than bitter, certainly richer. She'd never thought much of Richard and happily told me so as soon as we were divorced and hearing this latest news of mine she seemed to think it was only right to recount her own misfortune with the opposite gender, despite the fact I already knew the story well.

'Women like us are better off on our own,' she assured me, patting me gently on the arm.

Despite her best efforts, Aunt Lucy's pep talk wasn't making me feel a whole lot better and when Lou showed up, I could tell from my sister's expression that she feared her aunt had already caused irreparable damage.

'Aunt Lucy,' she cried, interrupting her flow.

'Louise,' Lucy beamed as though she hadn't noticed. 'Fantastic party,' she said. 'The garden's looking fabulous.'

'Glad you're enjoying yourself,' Lou replied. 'It's time to eat if you want to head over to the buffet.'

'Oooh, come on then Harriet. We want to get there before the queue builds up.'

'Actually we'll catch you up Lucy,' Lou replied for me before I had chance to say that I didn't feel hungry.

Lucy looked at us both and then winked. 'Yes, I'll leave you to it. I suppose you girls have lots to talk about.'

With a last grin she hurried off and dreading that I would enjoy the next conversation about as much as the previous, I hid my face in my wine glass and took another gulp.

'Fancy a paddle?' Lou said, looking sideways at me.

'Sure,' I shrugged, 'as soon as I've topped up my glass.'

She poured it for me and then we set off in the direction of the river which ran along the end of her garden. We would be alone there.

Lou was wearing a knee length, spaghetti strap red dress and kicked off her heels before sitting down on the wooden decking, and gasped as she dipped her big toe into the water.

'It's cold,' she smiled at me.

My feet felt uncomfortable in the ballet pumps I'd chosen to wear and so putting down my glass, I joined her, trying to hold back a little squeal as my feet recoiled from the cool water. Slowly they adjusted to the temperature and then I swept my feet back and forth through the river, listening to the comforting soft sounds it made and enjoying how it felt against my warm skin. Neither of us said anything for a while but my heart was beating fast and when I couldn't bear the silence any longer I broke it with tears. Lou shimmied closer and wrapped me in her arms and my whole body shook as she whispered smoothing words into my hair.

'I knew I shouldn't have worn mascara,' I moaned when I began to calm down.

Lou smiled and handed me a tissue. 'Here,' she said.

I dabbed at my eyes and sighed heavily.

'I heard about what happened,' Lou told me. 'All of it.'

'Who hasn't?' I spluttered. 'That Mrs Ellis has got a trap as loose as a leaky tap. And you don't have to tell me that I was an idiot, I already know that.'

'I wasn't going to say that at all,' Lou replied, looking almost hurt. 'I can't imagine how hard it must have been for you. I know I may have been a little...shall we say mocking at times, about you and your cats I mean. But I know Modi meant a lot to you and having lost him...well I don't think I can blame you for feeling shaken up. But I'm glad you didn't take Richard back,' she added carefully.

I covered my eyes with a shaky hand as the pain of more tears rattled my chest. 'Dan thinks I did,' I wept. 'I've made such a bloody mess of everything.'

Lou put her arm around me again and rested her chin on my shoulder. 'You called him?'

'More times than I can count,' I said. 'He doesn't want to speak to me.'

'But he must be hurting just as much as you.'

'Don't remind me,' I groaned. 'I feel so guilty all of the God damn time.'

'But you didn't do anything wrong.'

'I could have told Richard no straight away. I shouldn't have let it get that far.'

'Hardly a capital offence,' Lou sighed. 'If only you could make Dan listen.'

I could see that Lou was searching for an answer, certain somehow we could make it right again, but the cold, hard truth was that there wasn't one.

'He won't listen to me,' I told her. 'He doesn't believe me. I don't even know if I could look him in the eye now.'

'Of course you could. You love him don't you?'

Love. The word made me feel sick because I did, but he didn't love me back anymore and I told Lou so.

'But how do you know that if you haven't spoken to him?'

I licked a tear from my lip and began shaking my head. 'It's over Lou,' I said.

'So you're just going to give in?' she frowned. 'You don't even think there's a chance? No chance at all?'

Looking at her I thought of the gramophone and any answer I had stuck in my throat.

'I'll be all right Lou,' I eventually said. 'I've heard

time's the best healer.'

She brushed the hair from my face and squeezed my hand. 'Winning him back is the best cure of all.'

I tried to pretend I hadn't heard that. 'Why don't you head back to the party?' I suggested. 'Everyone will be wondering where their hostess has got too.'

'I'm only going if you're coming with me,' she replied. 'Besides, there's someone you need to talk to?'

'Who?' I frowned.

'Little brother,' she said.

'Ollie?'

Lou nodded. 'He's convinced it's all his fault.'

'But it isn't. Why does he think that? He didn't do anything wrong.'

'I've already tried telling him that,' Lou said, 'but it's not me he needs to hear it from.'

I sniffed and gave a firm nod. 'Okay, let's go.'

She pulled me to my feet and I wiped at my eyes again with the tissue.

'It's all right, you look great,' Lou told me.

I huffed a small laugh. 'Liar.'

Lou grinned. 'Well a few more smiles like that wouldn't hurt. They suit you, you know?'

'They're a little hard to come by these days,' I told her.

'But we're not giving up yet,' she said with a troublesome twinkle in her eye, the likes of which I used to see when we were young and she had a plan to get us out of a tight spot.

'Lou?' I frowned, but she wouldn't say anything else, just pushed my wine glass back into my hand.

'Come on,' she smiled.

TWENTY ONE

It was late before I caught Ollie alone. The band was playing a slow song and he, like me, had no partner to dance with and so sat watching from his table.

'Hey Ollie,' I said.

'Hey,' he smiled, twisting round in his chair. 'I was wondering where you were.'

'I was hiding,' I admitted, pulling back the chair next to his and sitting down.

He grinned but I could tell it was only skin deep.

'What do you make of them?' I asked, nodding towards the band.

'Good,' he said. 'And everyone seems to be enjoying themselves.'

'Yes,' I murmured as I glanced at the dance floor. Everyone but us anyway, I thought as I looked back at him. 'Ollie listen-'

'No, me first Hattie,' he cut in. 'I've been wanting to tell you that I'm sorry. I wanted to call you but I felt so guilty, I didn't know how to say it.'

'And I've been wanting to tell you that you have nothing to be sorry for,' I replied, stopping him. 'It wasn't your fault. None of it, do you understand?'

He started shaking his head. 'But maybe if I'd rang you sooner, if I'd noticed earlier that something was wrong, things might have turned out differently.'

'Ollie, if anything I'm just glad that,' I stumbled and broke off. 'I'm just glad that Modi wasn't alone and thanks to you, I got to see him one last time. That is all I could have asked for.'

Ollie was looking at the ground, his face hidden by shadow, and I reached for his hand.

'There is nothing to apologise for,' I repeated, knowing as he covered his eyes with his hand that I wasn't the only one hurting. 'I promise, Ollie.'

Slowly he pulled his head up, the candlelight reflected in his eyes, and smiling I hugged him. 'You okay?' I asked over his shoulder.

'Yeah,' he said. 'Yeah, I'm okay. What about you?'

I sighed and shrugged my shoulders. 'I've been better.'

'Do you want to talk about it?'

I shook my head. 'I'm tired of talking about it,' I said.

'Then what can I do to help?' he asked.

I looked back at the dance floor as the band picked up a lighter tune. 'You could dance with me,' I said.

He smiled and stood up. 'Yes, let's dance.' I took his offered hand and he squeezed it gently. 'We're in danger of not being invited to the next party if we don't smile a bit more. Yes, like that,' he said as I grinned. 'And I've got a few dance moves which should make you laugh even more.'

*

I was the last to get up the following morning and trundled downstairs with a heavy head. I met Tom in the living room and brushed the hair back from my face as I said hello.

'Feeling all right?' he asked with a knowing smile on his face.

'Yeah,' I lied. 'Could do with some tea though.'

'Well the others are in the kitchen and a pot's just been made.'

'Great,' I replied and I headed that way.

My mum, dad, and Lou were seated around the kitchen table and as soon as I pushed the door open, their animated conversation abruptly died.

'Am I interrupting?' I asked, halting as they all looked at me.

'No, no, not at all,' my sister beamed, but the moments awkward silence which had come before her answer told a different story. Quickly she got to her feet and hurried to the oven. 'Croissant?' she called over her shoulder.

'Sounds good,' I said, heading for a chair, and as I sank into it my mum poured me a cup of tea.

'Sleep well?' she asked as she passed it over.

I nodded. 'Yeah, thanks.'

Lou's kitchen was almost as big as the ground floor of my cottage and I watched as she zipped to and fro between the gigantic fridge and the marble worktop in her pink fluffy slippers. When she returned to the table she presented us with a large plate of warm crumbly croissants, halved and paddling in strawberry jam.

'Fantastic,' my dad beamed, whisking one from the plate.

Looking around the kitchen you would have been forgiven for not knowing that there had been a party at all last night. The empty wine and beer bottles were already gone. The glasses and plates were washed and back on their shelves and the air had a fresh, clean smell to it. That was Lou, I thought. Tidy and organised.

'Are we the last ones here then?' I asked as I picked up half a croissant.

'Yes,' my dad said. 'Ryan and Karen had to shoot back early, Ollie caught a lift with them.'

I nodded and licked some jam off my thumb. The atmosphere in the room was still unusually stilted and I wondered if I could prise any answers from them.

'So what's the plan for the rest of us then?' I asked.

'Oh, we'll start making tracks shortly after lunch,' my dad said.

'You don't have any other plans?'

'No,' my mum replied, shaking her head.

I frowned. 'What were you talking about when I came in then?'

'Just the party,' Lou said brightly. 'Just talking about the party.'

I looked at them each in turn but they all seemed very interested in what they were eating and not one met my eye. It seemed I wasn't to know, or at least not until they decided it was the right moment, and that moment came on the journey home.

'Harriet?' my dad said, glancing at me in the rear view mirror.

'Yes,' I replied, already suspicious of his tone.

'Your mum and I have decided to take you up on that offer of yours.'

My brow furrowed as I tried to think what he was talking about. 'What offer?'

'To take a short trip together, to the Lake District.'

I grimaced. 'Did Lou set you up to this?'

'No,' my mum insisted, twisting round to look at me. 'You were the one who suggested it, remember? On that postcard.'

'I remember,' I said quietly, putting my head back against the rest.

'Then what's the problem?' she asked.

'Say yes Harriet,' my dad smiled. 'I want you to show me all of those castles and ruined abbeys you told me about.'

'What you want is for me to talk to Dan,' I replied.

My mum put on a thoughtful face, as though she hadn't thought of that and was mulling it over. 'Well I suppose it would be crazy not too, whilst you were there.'

I sighed and looked out of the window. The idea had crossed my mind before, to go up there and see him, stand in front of him so that he had no choice but to listen. But what would I say? How many times could I say I was sorry, it was just a great big misunderstanding? And what were the chances that it would even change his mind? Would the whole thing just prolong my suffering because I didn't think I could bear to see him walk away again?

We got home before my parents pushed for an answer.

'I'm sorry,' I said, shaking my head as I stood outside my garden gate, bag in hand, looking back at them through my dad's open car window. 'I can't do it.'

I knew they were disappointed, it was written all over their faces, but as much as I hated to go back on my offer I just wasn't strong enough.

'Okay, we understand,' my dad eventually said with a

weak smile. 'But we're still going. If you change your mind there's always room in the car.'

I nodded. 'Okay,' I said. 'Love you.'

'Love you Hattie,' my dad replied. 'See you soon and keep that chin up.'

'Will do.' I smiled and stepped back, then waved goodbye as they drove away.

'Girls?' I called as I unlocked the front door. My heart was beating fast, trepidation coursing my veins. 'Girls where are you?' I dropped my bag and strode into the living room. 'There you are,' I grinned when I spotted them, all four curled up together on my armchair. Seeing me they began to wake up and one by one stretched their paws. 'Yes I missed you too,' I smiled as they all clamoured for my attention. 'It's good to be back home.'

'That looks so cute!' Charlie enthused when she got to the shop Thursday lunchtime.

'Thanks,' I smiled, stepping back to admire my work. I'd spent the morning creating a themed display in one corner of the room inspired by early twentieth century childhood. Over a table I'd put some vintage nautical print fabric and on top of that created a still life from baskets, books, and old wooden toys which I'd been collecting in my studio for weeks. A particular favourite of mine was the set of skittles painted to look like soldiers, and then behind the baskets I had stood a set of wooden shelves, each filled with little treasures reminiscent of a time long gone. Beside the table sat a rocking chair. I'd draped a quilt blanket over the back and then sitting quite happily in it, was a handsome Chiltern teddy bear.

'Is it finished?' Charlie asked as I tweaked what I'd

done.

'Almost,' I said and I added the last piece.

'You're selling the book?' Charlie looked surprised as I stood The Tale of Peter Rabbit in the heart of the display.

I nodded and then changed the subject. 'So how did it go?'

Charlie had been for a check-up about the baby and had a rosy glow to her cheeks.

'Great, everything's fine,' she beamed.

'That's fantastic,' I smiled. I was surrounded by empty cardboard boxes and picked up a couple.

'I bought a few things at the weekend,' Charlie admitted, grabbing one too. 'I found these adorable dungarees and the sweetest little hat. I swear I could have bought everything in that shop.'

I grinned and together we headed to the office. 'You can just put that anywhere,' I told her and then flicked on the kettle for lunch.

She dropped the empty box and sighed as she leant against the desk. 'I've never felt like this before,' she said. 'It's like I'm floating, like I'm dreaming.'

'Sounds magical,' I commented wistfully.

'I'm sorry,' Charlie apologised, shaking her head. 'I wasn't thinking. Let's talk about something else.'

'No, don't be,' I replied. 'I want to hear about it. I'm just a bit jealous, that's all,' I admitted, smiling again, 'but I'll get over it.'

We were both quiet for a short while and I reached for the box of tea bags.

'I'm going to miss you, you know?' I told her. 'When you leave.'

Charlie smiled. 'Don't be silly, you'll do fine without me.'

That all too familiar feeling of being left behind was creeping back again. Why was it that my life never seemed to move forward as everyone else's did?

Just then the doorbell rang and Charlie peered around the office door. 'Shall I get this one?' she said.

I looked through the gap as well. 'No, no, I'll go,' I said when I saw who it was rubbing their shoes on the doormat.

If I remembered rightly, the old lady's friend had called her Julie when she'd visited my shop all of those weeks ago, her eyes glued to the Elizabethan coffer, but today she came alone.

'Hello,' I said warmly after I'd left her to browse for a bit. She'd stopped in front of the coffer once again and was running her weathered fingertips over the smooth, dark wood. 'Can I help you?' I asked.

Julie looked up at me, her blue eyes sparkling, and with a wide smile she said, 'I'll take it.'

For a moment I wasn't sure that I'd heard correctly, I was so surprised by her immediate decision. I hadn't had to draw her eye to the particulars which made the antique special or negotiate the price. She didn't need convincing one bit that the coffer was what she wanted.

'Fantastic,' I smiled. 'You know I remember you from before.'

'And I haven't been able to get this beautiful coffer out of my mind since,' she grinned. 'I was so relieved it hadn't sold when I walked back through that door.'

'Your friend's not with you today?' I asked.

Julie wrinkled her nose and shook her head. 'I wanted to come alone.'

I read the rest between the lines.

'I find antiques are like men,' she said, stepping a little closer as though she were imparting a great secret.

'Sometimes they just catch your eye and you know that they've got to be yours, even when you get close enough to see their imperfections,' she added with a small laugh.

'I think we all have those,' I replied, smiling. 'I know I have.'

Having arranged payment and delivery Julie left, her smile undying, and I stood gazing at the coffer she'd just bought as her words echoed in my mind. I knew exactly what she'd meant. I'd felt that way myself more than once before. Sometimes you saw that piece, the one you knew you couldn't walk away from. From the very first glance you knew it was them you've been waiting to find and there's nothing anyone can say to change your mind. Not even the lies you try to tell yourself.

Suddenly realising what I had to do, I rushed back to the office and grabbed my phone.

'Dad?' I said when he picked up. 'I'm coming with you.'

TWENTY TWO

I took a deep breath and knocked on Dan's front door. I'd been building myself up to this moment for the last forty-eight hours and even though I'd run through my lines endless times, now I was here my mind was blank. I just wanted to turn around and run but I knew if that happened I'd only hate myself later so I stayed and reached for the wall to steady myself as I felt the blood drain from my face. When no one answered I knocked again, biting my bottom lip as I just wished he'd open up so I could get this over and done with. Then at least I'd know, one way or the other. After the third knock I decided no one was in and turned back to the car wondering what plan B was. It was a Saturday morning, not quite eleven o'clock, and the sun was shining. Perhaps he had Joe this weekend, I thought, and they'd gone out on the boat. It seemed as good an idea as any and so I headed for the lake.

As soon as I stepped onto the wooden pier, I knew my guess was wrong. I walked along until I came to

Dan's boat and then stopped and stared at it as it bobbed gently in the water. It had only been three weeks since I'd stepped aboard, holding Joe's hand, but it felt so much longer. I grit my teeth as I tried not to dwell on the memory. I felt heart-achingly alone without reminding myself of how happy I'd been then and tried to concentrate instead on where else I could find Dan. The café came to mind, the one in which we'd sat together not far from here and eaten ice cream as he'd pointed out his photos on the wall. I hurried back to the car and drove over there.

The café was bursting inside and out with tourists. Every seat taken, they were sipping teas, eating cakes or enjoying ice cream and although I highly doubted that Dan and Joe were amongst them, I still fought my way to the door so that I could check every table.

'Can I help you?' the woman behind the counter asked with a welcoming smile, looking up from the large sticky chocolate cake she had been in the middle of slicing.

'Actually,' I said, stepping up to the till, 'do you know these photographs-?'

'Dan Wilson,' she replied, cutting me off. 'He's the photographer and they're for sale, yes. Which one do you like?'

'Well I was hoping to speak to him myself,' I said.

'It's okay, we sell them on his behalf,' she beamed.

'No I mean, I know him,' I told her. 'I'm trying to find him. Do you know where he is?'

The woman seemed confused and subtly looked me up and down. 'Sorry love, I don't. I've got his number if you want it.'

'No, no,' I muttered. 'I've already tried that.'

I walked back outside and sank onto a wooden

bench. Now what, I asked myself. I was running low on courage, my optimism fading, and I don't know how long I sat there but it was the church bells chiming midday which abruptly stirred me back into motion.

'Of course,' I murmured out loud. There was still one place to look, one place I still might find him, but glancing at my watch, I realised I'd have to hurry.

This time there was no cat sitting on top of the post box and I had no postcards in my hand. Last collection on a Saturday was at half past twelve, I read and I glanced at my watch to find that I was a minute late. Had Dan already been and gone, I thought as I looked up and down the street. The minutes ticked by and I waited, my gaze eventually settling on a dove perched on the tiled roof of a log shed standing in the garden across the road, but my thoughts so much further away than that.

'Harriet?'

Hearing his voice I shot round. 'Dan,' I said, my heart suddenly quickening.

'What are you doing here?' he asked. He was taking small reluctant steps towards me, or rather towards the post box he was obliged to empty, and all the while he was frowning. It was obvious that he didn't want to see me and that stung like a fresh cut.

'You wouldn't answer my calls,' I replied meekly.

'Well there's a reason for that,' he retorted shortly and he pulled the keys for the post box from his pocket.

'Wait, hang on,' I interrupted, stepping between him and the box. 'Can't we at least talk about this?' I asked.

He pushed the keys roughly back into his pocket. 'What else is there to say? You cheated on me. You broke my heart. End of story.'

'But I never cheated on you Dan!' I insisted. 'Why won't you believe me? Look, I'm not lying to you,' I cried. 'Richard wanted me back and yeah, I did think about what he said. But are you telling me that if Joe's mum had come back to you, you won't have considered it? Not at all?'

He exhaled and his eyes were cold as he glared at me. 'This isn't about me Harriet,' he said. 'I loved you and I thought you loved me too. I trusted you. I wanted to...'

I could feel my cheeks burning red as he stumbled on his words and I could see that as he turned his head away, he was trying to control his temper.

'I wanted to spend the rest of my life with you,' he finished quietly. He wiped something from his face. I wondered whether it was a tear. 'I didn't realise I was just a stopgap for you, someone to make your ex jealous.'

'For Christ's sake Dan, it didn't happen like that,' I persisted. 'I didn't take him back. What do you want me to do? Get Richard here to testify? I know it looked bad, turning up at my house to find him there, but nothing happened. It's just that Modi-'

'Modi,' he interrupted, repeating the name. 'It's always Modi,' he said and there was something scathing about his tone. 'It's always about those cats for you isn't it? Harriet and her cats.'

He was staring at me again, taunting me, his words and the way he threw them at me cutting me so deeply. I couldn't believe what he was saying and suddenly I felt so ashamed for being the person I was, in the same way I'd felt ashamed before when people had so freely pointed their finger and called me a crazy cat lady. I never thought I'd hear those words leave Dan's lips but here I was, the tears rolling down my cheeks as he used the one weapon that he knew would hurt most. All those times he told me he understood, were they just lies?

'Do you mean that?' I said quietly, the tears reaching my chin.

He didn't reply. I heard the jingle of his keys and he walked around me, then unlocked the post box, but still I stayed there, staring at a manhole in the pavement until my tears washed it away into a watery smudge. It struck me then how this was all ending where it had started, and it had only started thanks to a cat who had been sitting on top of this post box.

'You know you're not the first,' I told him, struggling with my words as they raked my throat, 'to call me those things.'

He stopped moving and although he was turned away, I could tell he was listening.

'But you know what?' I said. 'I don't care anymore because I don't regret being who I am. I don't regret adopting those kittens and I don't regret going to Modi when he needed me either. But I do regret coming here because I've changed my mind; I don't want to love you anymore.'

I heard him shift his feet but I still couldn't see his face.

'I suppose I should thank you,' I said, 'for making it easier. Because the man I loved would never say those things.'

This was it; the moment when we said goodbye and never saw each other again. I opened my lips and tried to say it but the word would not come, as it had not the moment Modi's heart had stopped beating, and so I took a step back, then another, and with a third I turned my back and slowly walked away.

*

'Wow! Where have you been hiding that?' Charlie put down the beeswax polish and rag, and hurried over.

'Oh it's just something I found a while back,' I told her. 'I was thinking of keeping it,' I added quietly.

'I don't blame you, I love it. I remember my granddad used to have a gramophone. It wasn't as nice as this one though.' She glanced across at me then. 'What made you change your mind?'

I shrugged. 'I won't ever use it.'

'You prefer CD's to the old vinyls?'

That wasn't exactly what I'd meant but I didn't say so. It suited me not to go into any further details.

'Can I put one on?' she asked, keenly peering into the box of vinyls sitting on the table beside the gramophone.

'Sure,' I said, 'just not this one.' I took the vinyl that Dan and I had once danced to out of the box and took it with me to my workshop on the second floor. There was a lot to be done but as soon as I'd buried the disk in the bottom of my desk drawer, I ignored all of it and pulled over my sketch book. I flicked through the pages until I came to the two drawings I'd done in wax crayon and then I sat and stared at them with my head in my hands.

You don't want him back, I heard myself say. *Not after what he said. You tried to tell him the truth but he wouldn't listen. But you tried. At least you tried and now you know for sure.* The tears began to grow in my eyes and then fell down my face and at last landed heavily on the thick sketching paper. I watched a second fall and then another, and then roughly I picked up the whole book and threw it with my all my strength across the room. It landed nosily, pages strewn about and torn, amongst a heap of enamel jugs, but almost as soon as it hit the floor I rushed to my feet and gathered it up.

'Sorry Modi,' I whispered as I looked at his portrait, creased right across the middle. I tried to flatten it out and cursed for having lost my temper. Reaching for a couple of heavy books I hoped some weight on top of it would help smooth out the damage done, and then I went back downstairs.

'Where are you going?' Charlie asked once the customer she was dealing with had left.

'I'm just nipping out, I need some fresh air,' I said as I pulled on my coat. 'Can you manage without me for half an hour?'

'Of course, no problem, but it's raining,' she frowned.

'Don't worry, I won't wash away.'

She smiled gently then reached for something. 'Here, take my umbrella.'

'I'm only nipping to the supermarket Charlie, it's hardly far.'

'I don't care, take it anyway.' She pushed the umbrella into my hand.

'Thanks,' I said and I turned for the door.

'Harriet?'

I stopped and turned back. 'Yes?'

She had that look on her face, the worried one I'd seen so much of recently. 'Are you okay?'

'If I said yes you'd know I was lying,' I told her. 'You can always tell when I am. But you don't need to worry,' I added with a small smile. 'I'll be okay eventually.'

Charlie smiled, acknowledging the truth in what I'd said, and then I reached for the door handle, opened up the umbrella and walked out into the rain.

A shopping basket in one hand, I reached for a bag of chocolate buttons with the other and then a second. I was back to the ice cream and chocolate diet, supplemented each evening by a tear-jerker movie and glass of red wine, and I wondered how long I'd be able to get away with it before it showed on the scales. I tipped out my hoard onto the conveyor belt and a cashier with a warm smile said something about it looking like I was having a party tonight. How wrong she was, I thought as I smiled back at her. I shoved it all into a bag and then wandered back outside. The rain had stopped but a breeze was picking up and it tugged at my hair as I walked back across the car park. I was almost at the road before my gaze was snagged by the charity bin and glass bottle bank standing solemnly in the far corner of the car park, and I hesitated for a moment before changing direction and walking towards them.

I swallowed as I looked at the black bin bags and cardboard boxes piled up around the recycling bins, feeling a cloud of melancholia wash over me. I wasn't sure what I was doing, what I was even looking for. Modi wasn't here anymore, I told myself sternly. I was about to turn away when suddenly something moved. A box maybe? Yes, it was a box. I was certain it had shifted. Holding my breath I stepped up to it. Could it be, I asked myself, and I reached out with a quavering hand, slipped my finger under the lid and flipped it open. The anticipation in my heart died instantly when I saw that it was empty and when the wind pushed past me again, the box shook once more.

'Excuse me?'

I jumped. I hadn't known anyone was behind me and roughly I wiped at my eyes before turning round.

'Dan?' I gasped.

He looked nervous, but a hopeful kind of nervous, like the time our eyes had met across a busy Cumbrian pub.

'Hello Hattie,' he said, his words soft and warm.

'What are you doing here?' I said, my voice shaking as much as the rest of me.

'That girl, the one who works in your shop, she told me you'd be here,' he replied. 'I mean she told me you'd gone to the supermarket, she didn't specify the recycling bins. I saw you walk over here.'

He subtly peered past my shoulder and I could see he wanted to ask what I'd been doing kneeling amongst the boxes, but manners kept his tongue.

'This is where I found Modi,' I decided to tell him. 'I don't know what I was hoping to find coming back,' I added quietly, almost to myself.

'You miss him,' he said and it wasn't a question, just a statement of fact.

'I wouldn't expect you to understand,' I said rather coldly. 'I'm just a crazy cat lady after all.'

I could feel the anger in me steadily taking over and I wanted to shout at him, throw something at him, hurl some words which would hurt and bruise. But he could see it coming too and knew he had to get said what he'd come to say first.

'I feel terrible Harriet,' he said. 'I don't know what I was thinking. I was just so mad. I shouldn't have said all that, I didn't really mean any of it. I don't know where it came from and as soon as I said it I regretted what I'd done.'

He took a cautious step towards me and if it hadn't been for all the boxes around my ankles I would have recoiled back.

'I don't want you to come any closer,' I told him.

I wasn't sure if I believed he hadn't meant what he'd said but either way he'd said it and now every memory of us had been tainted by those words.

'Look, I was wrong not to listen to you when you tried to explain what had happened between you and Richard,' he told me. 'Perhaps I was wrong to just turn up at your house that day. I just wanted to be there for you, to help you. I know you're not a crazy cat lady,' he said. 'Perhaps a cat lady,' he added with a gentle smile, 'but a not so crazy cat lady.'

I could feel myself softening, even though I desperately didn't want to, and so when he stepped a little closer and reached for my hand I crossed my arms and angled my body away from him.

I could see him in my peripheral vision, hovering nearby, and I flinched when he gently touched my arm.

'I was wrong Hattie,' I heard him say, his voice not far beyond my shoulder. 'I was stupid, ignorant.'

His hand was heavier on my arm now and he was trying to turn me to face him.

'Don't,' I said, in a last defiant attempt to keep to my post. 'I don't want you.'

'And I don't believe you,' Dan replied, his other hand falling to my waist.

Locked in that limbo, I fought backwards and forwards with the demons in my mind, but when at last Dan heard me choke on my tears he pulled me closer and my heart pounding, I gave in trying to resist and twisting around in his arms, I buried my face against his chest.

'I'm sorry,' he whispered as he held me tightly, his strong hands on my back.

'Me too,' I said and I felt the warmth of his breath against my cheek as he bowed his head to mine. Slowly I pulled my face out of his t-shirt and looked up into his dark eyes. 'I never stopped loving you,' I whispered.

'And I'll never stop loving you,' he replied with a smile I had so sorely missed.

When I peeled away from him I looked up at the sky as the sun, having found its way through a chink in the clouds, bathed the corner of the car park in sunshine.

'There's something I need to do,' I eventually said, looking back at Dan as he interlocked his fingers with mine.

He looked at me curiously. 'What?'

'I need to head back to the shop,' I smiled. 'I've got to tell Charlie that I've changed my mind about that gramophone after all.'

About the Author

Catherine Walker was born in Staffordshire, England. A country girl, she loves animals and the great outdoors, and currently lives in southern France. *The True Story of a Not So Crazy Cat Lady* was short-listed in the Amazon Breakthrough Novel Award 2014.

To contact the author please write to;
walkercatherine@ymail.com

I'd love to hear from you.

You can also find
The True Story of a Not So Crazy Cat Lady
on Facebook.

10564669R00145

Printed in Great Britain
by Amazon.co.uk, Ltd.,
Marston Gate.